BEYOND 0'DARK 30

by

Edward M. Brittingham Captain, U.S. Navy (RET.)

RoseDog Books

PITTSBURGH, PENNSYLVANIA 15222

RoseDog Books
701 Smithfield Street
Pittsburgh, PA 15222
Visit our website at *www.rosedogbookstore.com*

ISBN: 978-1-4809-6192-0
eISBN: 978-1-4809-6213-2

DEDICATION

To my son-in-law, John Elwonger, for his interest and advice in preparing this manuscript.

To my loving and devoted wife, Joyce Brittingham, whose constant interest and help was invaluable to me.

Most of all, I dedicate this book to all who have ever worn the uniform and served honorably their country, the United States of America.

At the close of the 111th Congress, America is deeply in the bog of Thomas Jefferson's prophetic warning: "The enemies of the people are criminals and the government, so let us tie the second down with the chains of the Constitution so the second will not become the legalized version of the first." Unfortunately, the broken chains of the Constitution have failed to contain the federal government.

Scotty Starnes
January 2, 2011

CONTENTS

FOREWORD

Just when you think you have written your last book, so much happens that you know you need to write another one! So again, my husband has researched, filled countless legal pads with writing, typed endlessly, and spent much time alone and in thought.

Besides building a log cabin (a lifelong dream) at Lake Gaston, North Carolina, he serves as Commander of the Disabled American Veterans, Chapter 15, of Roanoke Rapids, N.C., is active in Military Officers Association of America (MOAA), and is active in our local church.

I am so very proud of my husband. I love traveling with him to book signings and meeting great people, and I am grateful to all who meet him, shake his hand, and thank him for his service to our country.

Lovingly,

His wife, Joyce Brittingham

PROLOGUE

Has the United States of America become a land of missed opportunity? Is this nation a land that lies to Congress when a felony is committed, whereas if it deceives us it is nothing but politics?

In the beginning of 2013, we were under the gun of sequester cuts. These cuts are to be secluded, withdrawn necessary plans that make our country less susceptible in keeping our country safe. Believe it or not, the president instigates these designed cuts.

This effort provides defense cuts, cutting back all arms, ships, submarines, and the needed manpower to maneuver these weapons to protect their country. Even the White House is on board by closing this facility without proper notice to all concerned.

Today we are plagued with many problems that may be revealed to the average American taxpayer. The start of the election of the president's second term began the downfall of the president's reaction to the polls. This coincides with the failure of answering questions of Benghazi directed on the president's shoulders of fixing accountable, the former secretary of state refusing to give her real, tangible facts on what caused the attack on September 11, 2001, and who failed to send help during the crisis, and still today many of these deserved issues are unanswered!

To tackle the new outrageous task facing our country demands each being on solid ground. The Internal Revenue has exploded its own fraudulent ways of taxation without representation! Spies are becoming more apparent with inter-operational men telling who, what, and when, all escaping from their own native land. This, of course, does not include the National Security Council or the Immigration eight Congressmen who are trying to get this passed. The message is simple: Read between the lines or connect the dots! Many of the elements of this piece pertain to the resolution of these happenings of the events listed in the table of contents.

Finally, the question arises, where was the president born? There are many topics, including birth and false claims, which could lead to disastrous outcomes to our president and to the status to our land, Constitution, and to the United States of America.

Beyond 0'Dark 30 was chosen as a title that symbolizes the trying times we have spent during President Obama's reign. The problems arose where the president claimed the killing of Osama Bin Laden as his main accomplishment. In all actuality, a Seal Team Six deserve the honor of eliminating his terrorist role.

New rules passed by Congress, new budgets, a second term, Internal Revenue Service headaches, National Security Agency problems, and the al Qaeda malicious attacks on Benghazi were paramount since the calendar year of 2008.

Alas, the president is acting through the secretary of defense by cutting the military services, men and women, ships, planes, submarines, and major shortfalls in all armed services. Can we survive with major cuts to the leader of all military forces?

CHAPTER 1

WHY ROMNEY LOST THE ELECTION

O ver coffee my sprit was dismal. The substance that gurgled down my throat was hot and did not destroy the woeful feeling in my brain. Governor Mitt Romney had lost the 2012 election, and all we had to look forward to was the coming four years in horror. Congratulations to all who pay no attention to the news, block vote by their ethnic background, vote on personality rather than the proven ability to govern, fall for unsubstantial claims such as "war on women," and you who were partying on college campuses instead of paying attention to what was really going on in our country. He must have engineered a senseless program that included many stealth tactics, such as abortion and giving out birth-control pills, to name a few stellar topics.

To step back, the Israel Nation News is usually to direct the Jewish vote. By analysis standards, the American Jews voted Democratic by 70%! Romney, on the other hand, failed to score among the voters. He did not lose because of Hurricane Sandy, which tore apart this area, nor did he run a weak campaign, and he did not go down into defeat because of members of the Republican putting up a better candidate. This candidate did not lose because the Democrats advanced with an uptick in the stock market. Romney lost because he did not have enough votes

Without a doubt, the Republicans were shell shocked as Mitt Romney faltered in the 2012 election. He had realized 322 Electoral votes, surpassing every battle-decisive state except North Carolina. The sign of the opponent's win went in favor of middle-class citizens of the United States. The culprit was the Latino and women voters, who were stronger and formidable ground games.

Media reports (Fox News) were a severe criticism for magnifying each Romney gaffe while not failing to treat his blunders fairly. When Obama stated, "You didn't build that," the media networks did not report that for four days. The Republican National Committee seized on these remarks, whereby

1

they used this for launching a new advertising blurb. This news counteracted on the Republicans because many voters turned on Romney by saying these words made them sway toward the president

One of the most bizarre steps of the ticket loss was the fact-checkers who did their jobs and obtained the truth over the Romney campaign statements. The General Motors closure at the GOP convention was, however, misleading. Romney and his cronies were, at this time, queried by his departures for meshing in dishonest attacks. Many say that Hurricane Isaac washed away the first day of the GOP convention and ended Romney's presidential ambitions. Senator Marco Rubio blamed the storm, which caused interruption/cancellation of a biographical video that was left out of primetime television convention coverage.

Clearly, the inescapable conclusion is that Mitt Romney was not known by the majority of American people. Willard Mitt Romney was born in 1947 and is an American politician and businessman who served as the Governor of Massachusetts from 2003 to 2007. Raised in Michigan by his parents, he attended the Mormon Missionary in France, beginning in 1966. He married his precious wife, Ann Davis, in 1969, with whom he fathered five sons. In 1991 he acted in both political races of his parents. He also earned a Bachelor of Arts degree at Brigham Young and completed a joint Juris Doctorate and a Master of Business Administration at Harvard University. He secured a position at Baine & Company, serving as CEO. In 1984 he handily spun Baine Capitol into great financial success that became one of the country's largest private investment firms. His net worth in 2012 was $190 to $250 million, which helped fund his future campaigns.

His political career was not stellar; in 1994 he ran for the U.S. Senate in Massachusetts and lost to Ted Kennedy. Being at Bain Capitol, he worked and became president of the Salt Lake Organizing Committee to originate the 2002 Winter Olympics, which opened a barrier for the springing forward of his political debut.

Elected Governor of Massachusetts in 2012, he turned the governing mass to a death-grip compromise. He enacted into law a healthcare plan that was the first of its kind in the United States. He took to modify the health insurance so that state level and individual mandates could obtain insurance. Governor Romney ran for president in 2008 and was bumped out to the race. The race for president and commander-in-chief was a close battle. His wife, Anne, was a strong advocate and rallied victoriously during his campaign. She was a vivacious woman who called each person to come together again to renew the effort to elect Romney President of the United States.

One reason why Romney lost the election was the giveaway "free" stuff. A powerful bargaining tool, the free goods are appealing to more and more people. Obama's land of the free is the place where this giveaway stuff is dispersed.

a.   Food stamps: 47,000 on this item recognize who they should vote for.

b.   Two full years of unemployment benefits, which cancels the looking for work and causes people to work off the books, collecting their unearned money. The idea of free birth control appealed to some for whatever dubious reason.

Infuriating as it may seem, Obama needed to portray his opponent as a voracious plutocrat who threw elderly women over a cliff. Romney is not grasping abruptly their life medication while starving the helpless and cutting taxes for the rich. What a bogus prevaricate! Still numerous disbeliefs are broadcasts including negative ads, but what really hurt Romney was the Hispanic vote. Romney thought he had this appeal concrete, but deep down inside the "free giveaway" made the difference in counting votes for the Demoncrats.

Another factor, as discouraging as it may seem, was the report by the Census Bureau. In the 2012 election, the miraculous downfall of the reemployment rate went from 8.1 % in August 2012 to 7.8% in September. The drop raised the eyebrows in the CEO world as he becomes an "unemployment rate truther" and brought serious thought because of his skepticism. The fact was that these numbers were being manipulated and the Census Bureau was aware of the fraud.

Many Republicans, as well as conservatives, were dissatisfied that Mitt Romney was a candidate for president but were insistent on retaking the House and Senate. That ladder of success is not reached unless Barack Obama is defeated. The United States is not dealing with a person with integrity but one who has single-minded goals and purpose dealing with narcissism! By his actions, words, and overall exploits at the end of four years, he does not wish to work with Congress. In his second term, Obama wants to force his so-called "radical" agenda on the American people through position of authority he has been granted. Conservatives, Libertarians, and Mitt Romney must come to grips with this moment in time, but all of Obama's resources have achieved controlling Congress and nearly all committee chairmanships.

Now the election was ongoing in November 2012, and those numbers were untrue and Jack Welch knew exactly what the fraud entailed. Two years before the election, the Census Bureau caught an employee fabricating the data that went into the report. Surprisingly enough, this infamitios exceeded one person, possibly more when President Obama was seeking election in 2012.

No president has ever run with an employment rate of 8.0%. There stood a made due number, and yet the Republican contender would have trumped over Obama. Romney, after months of scaling the unemployment rate and other major problems, would have edged the Democratic opponent.

So, in retrospect, who knows Mitt Romney? This perhaps is the dividing flag of the whole election. The Latinos had their minds made up. The young college kids depicted themselves behind Obama giving his campaign speeches throughout America, but they amassed behind him despite poor attendance. A deciding point in the 2012 election was during the town hall debate, when Obama utterly scolded Mitt Romney after he accused Obama of misstating the attack in Benghazi. Obama claimed it was a terror attack, but the ABC interview was not known to Romney or to any American people at that time. If Romney had stood his ground, the election would have been won by him. Romney's attempt was to bring up Benghazi before a national debate and the untold members of persons on whom Democrats counted who were deceased voters for a facade to be president.

NOTE: Russia is our Global Power opponent, and some analysts are asking if the United States is still in the Cold War. The foreign policy clash between the president and Mitt Romney on October 22, 2012, is in Romney's favor. Certainly the United States and Russia are entering a chilly period after a heralded "reset" button, because five years ago it was reset back to the Cold War!

Chapter 2

The Next Terrorist Attack

Since September 11, 2001, there have been a number of attempts to make America responsible for generating a target of horrific acts of violence. My mind remembers the Holy Scripture, which reports the word "violence" has the same meaning and interchanges with our word "terror." The books that were written over the past eleven years have produced almost five hundred versions of terror and created the type of man-style this person would involve. As in the United States the Muslims do not share our Christian beliefs, Fort Hood, Texas, November 5, 2009, is a prime example. Army Major Nidal Malik Hansan, MD, was a psychologist who believed his glory was to serve his natural religion. His orders were to cascade his overall diplomacy and strike out with "Allahu Akbar" and kill with weapons that eradicated thirteen victims. Even as we drag this obscene act many years past, his mutilated body paralyzed from his waist down, he is still being paid. Finally, he is on trial for the killing of these soldiers four years later. President Obama dictated this as a "workplace violence," not the insane, hateful project as it must be documented.

In the land of freedom, the stating of our country must be considered as the first ingredient of the next terrorist attack. The terrorist events did not stop in 2005; the Detroit Christmas attack followed by numerous attempts. Then there was the Boston Marathon debacle, which happened in early 2013. This stoned the Boston complex, and many people were decapitated a result of the bombs, which were known as "dirty bombs." This incident was called a Russian-made explosive, as it was learned by the older brother and brought over to the United States.

Today the Muslim radical is here in our country. Michigan possesses the maximum population as in other states, where the ethnic inhabitants are sparse. There are positive ways that the insurgent may sneak into our country. Yes, the drones are flying over the Mexican/Texas border. Drones are loaded with detection devices and are known to spot foreign people—yes, out of country, infuriating our land!

Seal Team Six took precise pleasure in the elimination of al Qaeda in Pakistan in May 2010. The Seals flew in helicopters into the area and prevailed the rule over the erratic Muslim factor. They arose from the dead and they branched out throughout the Middle East. This stabilized their being and ruled out the terrorist clan, but it is still operating. Now the previous clan is operating in the ring around the Middle East: Egypt, Syria, Yemen, Saudi Arabia, Lebanon, parts of Africa, and where you might expect it. Several sniffs indicate that Russia (KGB), Mexico, and Benghazi might be involved in specific cases or spastic intelligence gaps will be associated with violence.

The conflict of war and cultural innuendos has today dominated Jordon, Lebanon, and Iraq. The current battle continuous to fuse and the two major ideologies of Islam—Sunnis and Shiites—which have taken sides that may lead to a widing war. This could develop into a fear of chemical or genocidal war, according to the secretary general of the Syria Free Religious Scholars being a Sunni Muslim in Idlib, Syria.

Sunni Muslims are the majority in Syria. The royal families include those of Pierson Gulf oil owners who have landed behind the Syria rebels. Al Qaeda, who dominates this course, has ordered legions to the battlefront. President Assad, leader of the Syrian Shiites, has answered the plea, forcing Assad to defend his rule. Iran has deployed numerous troops, and the designated terror group Hezbollah in Lebanon is pouring armed forces into Assad's forces.

After the times of the seventh century, the battle beginning between the Shiite/Sunni occurred after the Islam prophet, Mohammed. The disagreement was that the father of Mohammed's wife would be the leader. But the other side believed his cousin, a blood relative, would be Ali, who should be the being optimal ruler. Today the offshoot is the Syrian choice. The majority of Muslims are relatively the same except Iraq, Lebanon, Bahrain, and Iran. Syrian Assab Alawite is a schismatic religious body and a direct choice of Shiite Islam. Will the upbringing of these countries' mutilation launch a terrorist attack on the United States? With the progress of Syrian conflict and the fierce battles over which ideology to follow, the need is for a better resolution to placate or passively bend these nations to peace before letting radical Muslims taint or spoil this mindset!

YEMEN
THIS IS THE HEARTBEAT OF TERRORISM,
AND IT'S RAISING ITS POWER TO THE WORLD

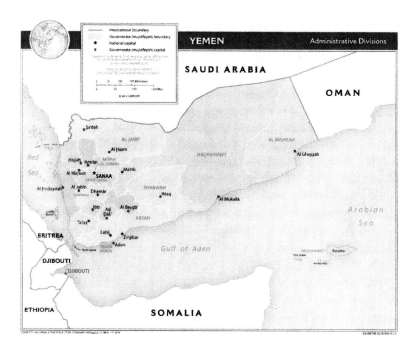

The militant Islamist group in the Iranian Arabian Peninsula (AQAP) was established in January 2009 with the pull of union Saudi and Yemen outgrowth. In the early 1990s, thousands of myahedeem estimated returned to Yemen after fighting problems in Afghanistan under Soviet occupation. With a base in Yemen, they started counterterrorism, which broke down the most active Qaeda affiliate, bent on attacking at both USA homeland and regional targets. The airline bomber on December 25, 2009, and a suicide bombing at Sanaa, capital of Yemen, underscored nearly a dozen Yemeni soldiers and in both instances achieved their objectives.

Yemen remains a fragile nation, yet the AQAP is expanding its capability to reign its power base in this country's south. Yet the United States is keeping particularly the drone strikes in the area. Yemen faces challenges that force the period of uncertainty. Forty percent of their people live in poverty. Essentially Yemen is facing a food crisis, which was reported in 2013. With the new government of president, Hadi is a weak, flamboyant atmosphere, which means deviation of a two-year process that was outlined in the Yemen *Observer*. There some goes for the military.

The Countering Terrorism Center is a good start, but all plans enjoy more support than AQAP. The United States paid little attention to what was going on until the attacks on the USS *Cole* and 9/11 happenings. The steps following this message marred the strategy that led to short-term combating AQAP, boosting development assistance and developing international support. In 2010 the U.S. Department issued sanctions on financial support for terrorism organizations. Secret drone bases in at least the Arabian Peninsula were U.S. reactions to Yemen insolates. As recently as 2012, drone strikes are on an upward slope.

Even with all of the targeting and killing of extreme Muslims, there is still a central component that dictates counterterrorism operations in this country. The prospect for more al Qaeda in this Arabian Peninsula is increasing no matter what the Yemeni Government does; jihad still has the upper hand to this rural area's multiple outcome.

The United States State Department describes Iran as an overwhelming active state of terrorism. Iran has been in all countries that have represented a banker that has financial regions from Lebanon, Hezbollah, in the Middle East, to Palestine, and some are worried about what Iran is doing south of Iraq. After the fall of the Shaq in 1979, the Iranian Revolutionary Guard (IRGC) was established by Iran. This force was to equalize the social policy of the government. The IRGC, termed *Pasdarun-e Inqulab*, had ties with underground operations in the Middle East. The predominant group of this band is made up of twelve thousand Iranians, Afghans, Iraqis, Lebanese Shiites, and North Africans. Many of these legions have trained in Iran. The Hezbollah faction provides intelligence, logistics, and operational units in Lebanon. In August, Ayatollah Ali Khamenei increased their efforts in terrorist training as their interests were given signs of warning by both the United Nations and the West's support of Syria.

The bottom line is this: Iran is offering help to Iraq to pacify its civil physical force. The major thought in life is the Americans will not succeed in this land. Therefore the input and training will restore security and hold steady Iraq. The assessment of terror attacks is high when Iran is ready to launch an atomic weapon; it is high on the list of strikes from this country. In congressional meetings conducted recently, it forecasted that Iran has crossed a threshold with the United States. This country has been linked to targets overseas, especially the role of a plot to assassinate the Saudi official in Washington, D.C., approximately a year ago.

National Intelligence James Clapper indicated that the movement about illustrated that some Iranian prominent, including the Supreme Leader, have reoriented their brainwaves. Movements within dictate they are more likely to attack the U.S. in response to actions that threaten the regime!

AFRICA

Africa as a whole continent is plagued with a worldwide campaign concerning terrorism. It is puzzling to verify the threats from the Horn, and last of Africa an area of action is the sparsely populated areas such as Sahel, where groups such as Salafist Group of Preaching and Combat can find refuge and develop training camps. Perhaps the most challenging of all, Nigeria, is the political and economic shortfalls. One hundred thirty million people are in some form of terror or in a state of extreme panic. In summary, all parts of Sub-Saharan Africa based on all public diplomacy must be watched.

The U.S. has shown favorable to this part of Africa by allocating a pledge of one hundred million dollars of donations for counterterrorism assistance from President Bush. This money filtered down to other nonessential programs that have been recommended that a force on east Africa be incorporated in our antiterrorism budget. In Kenya, once again the U.S. backed movements in this providence. The fighting resolved a new strengthening of government and will be aware of any political backlash as Kenya presents a strong being in the war on terror.

There is a pulling back and forth in Nigeria over the Muslim population. Introduction of Shiara has taken hold of seventy-two of Nigeria's thirty-six states. Growing Christian activities have vaulted terrorism between Muslims. The dispute has finally ended with the final stages of World Health Organization programs to do away with polio worldwide. Down under in Nigeria, Osama bin Laden himself was a priority-one target! Oil is in the delta region, where the bulk of the oil industry and the American investment is located. It is difficult to measure why the American is not present in this Muslim-dominated north country, there are no daily programs of diplomacy, and there is no capacity for metering trends of Islamic control. A new interest and action that is moving faster than a speeding bullet across the Sahara desert is the Pam Sahel initiative. U.S. satellites have been illuminating and have shown training sites that are serving to indicate threat that these countries have been inflicting on its troops. Now the U.S. has become a critical player.

As we mull over all of these disturbances, we are all compelled to shut down this tidal wave of terrorism. Nigeria, Libya, and the Horn of Africa is in a titanic mess. Our (USA) interest is paramount, and then and only then will strategic help meet and dominate the terrorist threat on the mainland.

UNITED STATES OF AMERICA

Finally, the Boston/ Soviet Union terrorist connection. Two brothers bombed the Boston Marathon, and where Russia fits into the equation is that the older brother went to Chechen Muslims in Russia to make the two or more pressure cookers with gunpowder and enhance their kill rate with the addition of nails and metal balls. The pressure-cooker bombs were hidden in backpacks and were remotely detonated using the battery of a remotely controlled toy. Apparently the older brother went to Chechens to learn how to design and make the bombs. Amazingly the making takes very little engineering background. The link between the perpetrator and the main clue was identifying the bomber. Are Islamic extremists attempting jihad against the United States? It's too soon to tell that the Russian government will not prevaricate about this incident; however, it tells of several practicing Muslims in Chechens.

At the Senate Intelligence Committee last week, the Director of National Intelligence testified that the threat of terrorism is not any less than a decade ago. After a trillion dollars spent on fighting terrorism have received no gains, it was a powerful blown statement!

Director Clapper would want us to believe that al Qaeda is a morally or intellectually more powerful than before. War on terror, both government and industry, economic pressure, has affected military/intelligence, in high threat levels without explaining them due to secrecy, is best to keep our security budget untouched.

More likely, the government's increasing policies are promoting al Qaeda to group to arise when initially the previous camps were destroyed by drones or military attacks. A former State Department Official said that every drone attack in Yemen results in the creation of forty to sixty new enemies.

Clapper also inerates that Syria has the al Qaeda taken in a new member, Al Nusra Font, which has for a fact attacked the homeland. Unfortunately we are sending weapons to the Syrian rebels. The Saudi "allies" are supplying the same rebels that we are supplying. Is the United States of America setting up the Al Nusra Font for the next terrorism attack on the U.S.?

Well, you decide. Yemen is the next attempt of the attack of terrorism on our native soil.

CHAPTER 3
A NUCLEAR IRAN AND OTHER COUNTRIES

SYRIA – A WAR-STRICKEN AREA

Greatly involved in the Syrian uprising is President Bashar al Assad, head of the Syrian Nation. Hezbollah, pronounced "Hizbullah," is a Shia Islamic Militant group and is more powerful than the Lebanese Army. He has joined hands with Syria in this, shall we say, civil war. Hezbollah was convinced by Muslim clerics and was funded by Iran following the assault of Israel in Lebanon. Since that shortfall, Lebanon had been funded and groomed by the Iranian Revolutionary Guards, which fortified their force with excellent training.

Hezbollah contains a high profile, as he is embroiled in the Syrians' civil war. Waved on with enthusiasm, a convoy of the infectious forces headed into the region—the mission obviously a secret. He is fighting more in view of defending the conquest where President Assad, a fellow Shia, is now clashing armor in an increasing secretariat conflict against Syria's Sunni Muslim advantage. Hezbollah charged the conflict head-long, sending his forces to assault the Syrian Army, taking the city Quasar from rebel control. Using his guerilla expertise, they forged a ground invasion, which forced the rebels to scatter and flee.

The rebels sought a new way to win some accomplishments, not from the stronghold of Hermel. The low-rise concrete houses were near the border; this was where Kalashnikob-loyoed yellow flags marks the street corners. Many shells were fired into Lebanon by the Syrian rebels, who left many newly painted martyr placards showing Hezbollah men had died crossing the border.

Israel came to play in the debacle when it attacked a rare airstrike that destroyed a convoy, which contained anti-aircraft weapons bound for Hezbollah, a militant in Lebanon. This definitely was a blow to the civil war. Regional officials thought the shipment included SA-17 anti-aircraft missiles, which would cause Hezbollah to have purchased "game changing" weapons. These military rockets could knock down helicopters or even jet fighters. President Assad was upset that further destroying of this kind could strike back with chemicals or some form of advanced weapons.

In May 2013, a British Consulate visited Syria in pursuit of chemical weapons. The confidential mission that he was to investigate was the nerve agent sarin used in those Syrian cities. For the United Nations inspectors, this inquiry had cropped up back in Iraq, where they scoured Iraq's deserts and playground parks more than a decade ago. Evidently they were looking for vast stockpiles of chemical weapons, which were long destroyed or no longer existed. Much time was contemplated over whether Syria was involved in the exchange of chemical weapons.

Syrian rebels scored a strategic victory since the outburst of what had involved. Rebels led by al Qaeda-linked militant groups led by Jabaat al Nasea now controlled the water of the al Furat dam. Officials say that misuse or causing a flood from the dam could overflow into many of the providences in Syria and Iran. This action began on the Euphrates River, where two dams were seized. Behind al Furat dam is Lake Assad, which is the largest water reservoir. Additionally this dam produces eight hundred eighty megawatts of electricity, which is small especially when Syria depends on plants powered by oil and basic fuel oil. When the rebels stormed the town and the dam, they set ablaze the giant statue of President Horfez Assad, the father of the present ruler of Syria.

Experts say that detecting the use of chemical weapons becomes more difficult as time passes. If the United Nations team ever thinks of returning to Syria to find these sites, the job will be even harder. Iran has joined the Syrian mass by sending its soldiers to fight alongside President Assad. As of now, an unknown number of fighters have been sent, yet no positive numbers are assessed. Syrian forces have been claiming that battle-worn civil troops are fighting hand to hand with Hezbollah to not let Syria fall.

Secretary of State Kerry is on a dual mission in order to prosper talks between the force and the rebels. Recently a U.S. Senate panel voted to provide materials to the rebels, including weapons, which would represent an aggressive step regarding the civil war. Pressure is mounting on whether the United States is ready to alleviate its status quo outlook on a two-year-old civil war in Syria. Despite a degree of enthusiasm favors, the White House, et al, events are rapidly hastening the strategic parallels, whereby the Americans appear to become involved in this conflict. With the "Red Lines" being crossed to our president's degree, this has the setting of whether chemical gas has been used by the Syrians against the al Qaeda rebels. Weapons could wind up in the wrong hands. This could be the risky chance of our weapon-fitting armor. The rebel forces the U.S. supports are unkempt, disorganized, yet they are somewhat extremist Sunni Arab groups that were killing our forces in Iraq! Officials are studying the matter, which could mobilize the mission first by various sizes and scopes of the mission, knock out air defenses, and ground artillery strikes would lead to a clear safe zone to a nearby country.

On March 10, 2003, Iraq moved weapons of mass destruction to Syria. Ha'aretz has reopened the ability of finding weapons of mass destruction in Iraq. Satellite photos found a site in Syria that, when reported, it shocked the world with his reporting that Iraq's weapons of mass destruction (WMD) had been moved to Syria on March 10, 2003, before the U.S. invasion commenced. The site is near Masyaf, Syria, which has five installations and has leading underneath the mountain. This confirms Nizor Nayorif, who said in 2004 that his sources were true, in that Saddam Hussein's WMD's were in Syria.

One of the three areas was reported as being underneath al Baida, north of Masyaf. One of the co-writers who reported this noted that relatively large aircraft could handle these chemicals into Lebanon. Another site was Bekon

Valley, where it may be another location to house Iraqi weapons. Many men, obviously engineers and dedicated chemical experts, were consumed that their work was not WMD in Iraq. Many loose ends were discussed by some, yet when reported fifty trucks crossed the border on March 10, 2003, and this verified that Syria had the weapons of mass destruction. The National Director went to jail, for testimony that he spoke to about forty Iraqis who professed that weapons of mass destruction were going to Syria by convoys between February and March 2003.

As explained in detail in Ken Trummerman's book, *Shadow Warriors*, a high-level meeting was convened February 10 through 12 2004. Officials from the United States, the UK, and Ukraine were present at the conference. The Ukrainian body provided the Russian effort, including a plan of intervention and even Russian Spetsnaz Officers who were used. Ion Pacepa offered a Soviet plan (Operation Sarindar), where they would cleanse rogue states of any evidence that the West would question about the weapons of mass destruction. This knowledge perpetuated the use of Soviet advisors in Iraq before the United States invasion, which is a strong indication that some of these individuals were presented medals from Sadaam Hussein, leader of Iraq at that time.

Another federal agent, Dave Gaubatz, deployed to Iraq, told that the WMD had been moved to Syria with the aid of Russian Intelligence. Iraq personally told of Russian presence before the American soldiers arrived in Iraq.

The President of the United States has announced that Syria has used chemical weapons during 2012 and 2013. This chemical, known as the nerve gas sarin, has been used multiple times. Approximately one hundred or so people have perished from this burning poisonous or asphyxiating gas. This obviously crosses the "Red Line" that was established the previous year. The White House later said they would support the Supreme Military council in Syria, but will this necessitate military support?

Many senators and congressmen are upset with the current crisis and bloodshed, and this chemical warfare is only a symptom of future war in this land. This dragging of human sufferance into the third war of killing is uncalled for. But there are fastidious factors we foresee that complicate this action. Namely, the U.S. has worked its way into a tickelous relationship with Russia. This means not to apply pressure on Assad's period of rule. Some officials of the U.S. Government have indicated that arms supply to the rebels could fall into the hands of others.

Now the White House has reliable evidence that Syria has used chemical weapons. This does not come as a surprise! Previous reporting of the Iraq-

Syrian transfer of these deadly chemicals is a nemesis to the human race, whether the Assad forces or the rebels deny the charge of dispensing this horror of death. Reports of the use of sarin gas were centered around the Aleppo providence in the Damascus area. This will cross the "Red Line," which President Obama has made, if it is clear that these weapons, if discussed, will be held accountable.

Iran has joined the Syrian mess by sending its soldiers to fight alongside President Assad. As of now, an unknown number of fighters have been sent, yet no positive numbers are assessed. Syrian forces have been claiming that battle-worn civil troops are fighting hand to hand with Hezbollah to not let Syria fall.

Officials are studying this matter, which could mobilize the mission first by various size and scope of the mission, knock out air defenses, and ground-artillery strikes would lead to a clear, safe zone to a nearby country. Therefore, clear and present danger remains for our "boots on the ground." The president made this decision at present, but the eagle has a wary eye!

Quick as a flash in one month's time, June 22, 2013, the U.S. has been secretly training the Syrian rebels. Central Intelligence Agents and Special Forces have been training these rebels with anti-tank and anti-aircraft weapons since last year. Last year President Obama approved plans to make this happen. The covert U.S. training bases located in Turkey and Jordan will likely provide additional arms, ammunition, and ultimately heavier weapons. At the outset, the rebels say they lack sufficient science of weaponry to gain the offense in the bitter, sadistic civil war.

The training involved a Free Syria Army, which is a rebel group. The number of rebels appears to be twenty to forty-five insurgents in Jordan. Special Forces selected these men, who will be given nonlethal guidance, along with uniforms, radios, and medical aid. The two-week course includes Russian-designed anti-tanks as well as anti-tank rifles. The training started in November 2012, and over one hundred rebels are now in the fighting in Syria. The rebels, however, were promised armor-piercing weapons to gain an advantage over Assad. The arms shipments pass through Qatar, Saudi Arabia, and other countries.

Islam extremists group in Syria with al Qaeda ties identify and train Americans with other Westerners to carry out attacks when they have returned to America. Although these efforts are in the early stages, for Libya it means that Europe and the United States will fight tactics with the rebels against the government of President Bashlar al Assed. Approximately seventy Americans have traveled and returned a qualified Jihad tactical weapon. The director of the FBI said that tasking is one of the highest counterterrorism priorities. Round-the-clock surveillance has been the investigator's mission, and he wanted to know exactly how much the Jihadists know and transmits this information to the attendees of past Syrian training.

Most of the Americans who have traveled there are lost or are killed in training. American officials are worried about the intelligence gained from the travel records and other sources who have had experienced a need for traveling to Syria.

This recent move by the U.S. has suffered blows by the Soviet Union. Russia states the U.S. is employing a "disaster" for this two-year war to end. Russia and the United States are on a stalemate after the rebels get support.

The Syrian rebels accused of releasing chemical weapons was the theme of today. A detailed report estimated that 355 deaths were attributed to a chemical attack in a suburb of the capital called Ghouta. Meanwhile U.S. Naval units are closing this country, as the U.S. is considering an attack on Syria. Of those who died, the rebels who were blamed for the gas said the Syrian government had proof of their responsibility but without giving details. In Turkey, top rebel leader Commander Salim Idris said opposition forces did not use chemical weapons Saturday and the regime is lying.

Secretary of State John Kerry proved there was undeniable evidence that a large-scale chemical attack strongly pointing at Bashar Assad was the culprit. John Kerry said, "By any standard, it is inexcusable." Russia condemned the idea of intervention from the West. An attack on Syria would create more bloodshed. Most likely the U.S. Navy ships would fire tomahawk cruise missiles into this country. In Capitol Hill, the bipartisan support appeared to be increasing.

President Obama's present goal is a "Red Line" against chemical weapons. France released an intelligence report that verified the use of chemical weapons. The Syrian Assad said that it sparked an uncontrollable regional conflict and spread "chaos and extremism." Russia, along with Iran, has been a staunch supporter of Assad. President Vladimir Putin suggested sending a delegation to the U.S. to discuss the situation with Congress.

Vladimir Putin warned the West against taking action or one-sided action in Syria. He stated that poison gas was used on his own people and was not definitely approved. Putin has stated that components of S-300 air defense missiles to Syria have frozen. He suggested that Russia may sell to other countries. From Putin himself, it is assured that regular armed forces have encircled the rebels. Furthermore, he (Assad) would use chemical weapons, using the rule of force. Putin used the same mass destruction of Iraq in 2003 to justify this invasion, whereas Obama stressed that relations with Russia (Putin) had "hit a wall."

President Obama reveals that he will siege on Syria until the last attempt so that the U.S. must retaliate because of the nation's use of chemical weapons effort fails. He entertains the potential of removal of all threatening chemical weapons.

Russia's proposal is to place them under international control for dismantling and a lengthy difficult plan, not to mention the inventory. Syria is believed to have one thousand tons of weapons transferring from fighting ranges, which presents a logistical and security poison ivy itch! Assad is sometimes called a "devil in the details." The organization for the prohibition of chemical weapons is working on details that provide development, stockpiling, and the use of chemical weapons. Destruction is problematic, however, as a secure facility to carry out this hell-bent task.

The White House has tried to pin the diplomatic opposition on chemical weapons on Russia rather than the U.S. However, the threat of a large transfer of chemical weapons and its decimation of them presents a big problem to not only the Syrian people, but also to the neighbors in the countries nearby. While removing the explosive load, there has yet to be a plan to culminate Syria to release its chemical weapons stockpile. Assad says he will schedule chemical weapons if the U.S. stops threats and aid to the rebels.

The U.S. and Russia have agreed to work on the UN Security Council Resolution to insure verification to insure, destroy, and break apart these weapons stockpiles. President Obama retains his right to unleash military strikes to defend security and absence of UN authority. Syria has until Saturday to list its gas or chemical weapons. All of these weapons stockpiles, material, and equipment must be put to an end according to a place recently devised. The team of inspectors enters in November 2013, when the stockpiles should be destroyed by mid-2014, but this is now Friday's inspection. There are forty-five sites associated with chemical gas. Reports are that some are located near Damascus, while others may be found near Aleppa and in the West Coast near Latakia.

The rebels believe that the U.S.-Russian deal, whereby Syria is to relinquish these chemical gases, leaves Assad as he eludes a new confidence in this aftermath. Rebel and Commander General Solim stated that Syria and its ally Russia of "marking time" in order to pass the time away. Thus, the United States has tried to get UN support, but it will not use force against Syria if it does not cough up its chemical weapons!

The UN reported on September 17, 2013, that rockets with nerve agent sarin have been fired from within Assad forces near its military bases. President Obama cleared the way to send assistance to Syria. A senior advisor said that the training would not give preparation to move or to destroy.

Russia indicated that the UN Security Council resolution left Syria's handling of weapons did not allow the use of force; it suggested that it could change if Damascus changes the deal to not give up the stockpiles! This plan calls for an inventory of all stores within a week with all necessary documents/weapons out of Syria destroyed by 2014. A U.S. retaliation or a military option remains on the bargaining table. Finally, a deal is reached by five members of the UN Resolution.

The UN Security Council voted all together to secure and destroy Syria's weapons of mass destruction in order to take the poison gas off the area of engagement. This decision will eliminate this chemical arsenal by mid-2014. This resolution called for an easement of these conditions if Syria failed to comply. Russia, on the other hand, gives his ally the means to stop any punishment for being realized. We have inspectors who will provide updates regarding seven areas that were not listed, four more than were previously recorded.

The Syrian government will not accept a "so-called" transition peace initiative that excludes Assad and Foreign Minister Walid-al-Mollen, reported the Associated Press. The Syrian opposition exacerbated by two and one half years of bloody fighting, which prevents Syria from establishing a translating government with full executive rule. The regime denies carving out a brutal viable campaign against many homeland people concerned about a nerve gas attack that left hundreds dead. Iran has been a key supporter of Assad, yet this had not hurt the Iranian-U.S. relations over the past two weeks.

The Syrian prime minister pledged to cooperate with the dismantling of chemical weapons but vowed to crush a revolution that has gained mass resistance from al Qaeda and other international Jihadists. Muslims stated that the rebels included fighters who would display barbaric extremism and would dismember bodies into pieces while alive and send their limbs to their families. The Syrians' war against terrorism will return to their countries, which means no land will be immune, nor borders, nor limits of geography. Syria and Russia, her arch ally, have believed the rebels for an August 21, 2013, attack.

Vladimir Putin's Russia has slid and remains a Cold War contact with the U.S. Obama saw more rhetoric displayed by the Soviets with day-to-day talks overshadowing differences between Syria and the missile shield in Europe. President Obama said the symbolic one-on-one eventuality grants up a temporary asylum for Snowden.

IRAN'S QUEST FOR NUCLEAR POWER
IRAN – THE POSSIBILITY OF A NUCLEAR WEAPON

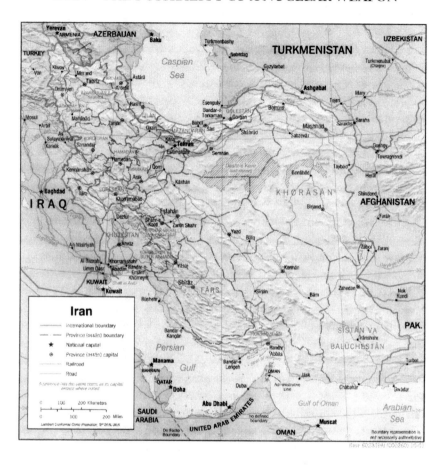

The nuclear evolution of Iran commenced in the 1950s with the help of the United States of America in accordance with the Atoms for Peace Program. This help from Western Europe and the U.S. continued until 1979, which sparked the Iranian revolution that caused the fall of the Shaw of Iran after the revolution of the clandestine program of research into nuclear weapons was destroyed by Ayatollah Ruhollah Kohomeini. He considered this program forbidden under Muslim law. Iran later repudiating possession of weapons of mass destruction.

Iran's first nuclear plant was named Bushr I reactor with Russian assistance and was opened on September 12, 2011. Iran has said that a 360-MW facility would be located in Darkhowin, Iran. Atronenerqoprom, the Russian engineering company, indicated that the plant would reach full capacity by the end of 2011. Iran also stated that it would seek other medium nuclear power systems and more uranium mines for the future.

In 2007 the Iranians had the capability, though not in the eyes of the United States Intelligence community. In 2012 the same agency reported that Iran was pursuing research that could enable it to produce nuclear weapons, but the indications were she was not attempting to do so! In November 2011, the top blew off and the International Atomic Energy Agency (IAEA) criticized Iran that she had secretly worked toward development gearing to a nuclear weapons capability. This IAEA report details many studies related to nuclear weapons designs, detonator development, multi-point initiation of high explosives, and experiments with nuclear payload inter alia with payload into a missile delivery vehicle Iran, but of course, threatened to reduce cooperation with the IAEA.

On October 25, 2013, the Obama Administration showed a widening gulf with key Middle East allies over talks about nuclear Iran, Israel, and the Persian Gulf Arab leaders concerned over drastic shortfalls to Iran's atomic superstructure! Teheran has insisted it will never accept this plan. The difference came as Israeli Prime Minister Benjamin Netanyahu claimed to lecture Secretary of State John F. Kerry. His warning was against a dead argument that would allow Iran this capability to make enriched uranium, i.e., the final step to a nuclear weapon. "Iran must not have a nuclear weapons capability, which means they shouldn't have centrifuges for enrichment." In essence, there was a combination of strict curbs and continually monitoring of its use so that it cannot make nuclear bombs. Kerry's view of this situation is that the Israelis' deal will not come as the security and other close nations are at stake.

Iran's president, Hassan Rouhani, said this day that the world power, including the United States of America, has yielded to the "Iran's nations' will." What this means is the deal is confirming a six-month gift that will allow the Iranian regime to continue its advanced centrifuge program, meaning it's beginning to develop a nuclear plant in Arak, Iran. Meanwhile President Obama told Americans to give peace a chance with the deal. This, plus the backhanded ploy of the Iranian president can rapidly lead to a nuclear bomb!

At the crux of the disagreement is whether a deal can be struck that allows enrichment of uranium for non-weapons programs. The only fail-safe solution to this dilemma, according to the Israelis, is the dismantlement of Iran's enrichment infrastructure.

EGYPT
EGYPT – A COUNTRY THAT NEEDS TO BE WATCHED

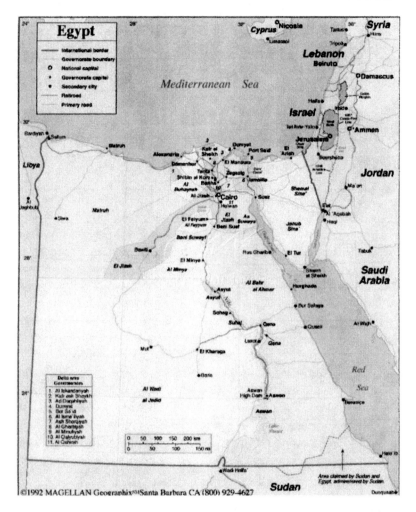

The United States will carry out the current agreement long past to give Egypt 16 F-16 fighter jets plus tanks. The final four jets will be delivered in the coming weeks. Secretary of State John Kerry states this may be put on hold in view of present turmoil. Washington has refused to label former Egypt President Morsi as a coup. There are many details that sway his removal of power.

Under U.S. law, the stoppage of $1.5 billion in aid and halt the delivery of jets, if it confirms a coup occurred, Egypt is only served in aid received from the U.S. $650 million in military aid and yet it is to receive $585 million more

21

due by September 2013. The Muslim Brotherhood insisted that U.S. support directly supported Morsi from power. The Brotherhood states that the integrated support is being initiated in recognition of the coup.

Egypt's military officers seized power after three decades under British occupation and promised to return to the barracks six months later. Gomel Abdel Nassar began to build up to the country's strong man after a power struggle with an older officer. Anwar Sadat succeeded him in 1970, where he concentrated on power, thereby marketing his grip on power or "corrective revolution." Marbarak began his rule of almost three decades with a series of goodwill antics that would release hundreds of Sadats' bad-mouth persons with a promising and democratic gesture. He dedicated to the last two terms with Gomal, his son, standing by. The freshly void graffiti representing Mohad Morsi tells in high hopes that barely six months after assuming power as the first democratically elected president, the Islamist has abandoned his pledge due to governmental and authoritative ways. In the past three weeks, with a multitude of measures he has given himself absolute power. His actions have a tremendous effect with a one-man power grip. This is the Egyptian way of thinking involving when the leader is pretending to be God!

In Marsi's choice, his observers believe his actions derive from the Muslim Brotherhood. In the final assessment, he is a dictator. After he was acclaimed president, he will follow the will of the Brotherhood. The Brotherhood has been in existence for sixty years. The oldest is Islamist convention. Now it has emerged as Islamist Shariets throughout the Egyptian region. The Muslim Brotherhood is confined struggle with compelling general as to how the influence with the army will have to take over the civilians in a quarter of a year. The agreement is over a new constitution, which was drafted by an Islamist-like body that builds around the new president. What army privileges will remain, and how much is the military retraining in power over the national security issue?

Islamists are engaged with the liberals in that they walked out because they felt the Islamists have too much weight and turns off or does not represent Egypt's diversity. In other words, the party with majority must form the government. The government must succeed and be in the arms of Parliament. The army/chosen body first raised the issue in late November by giving a broad remit over national security. The Islamists fumed and turned their suggestion down. The Egyptian army feels it will lose control to the Islamists as well as other functions that will be vital throughout. For example, the army receives $1.3 billion per year of U.S. Military Aid, according to a program in 1979. This must be maintained!

The brotherhood respects all of these treaties. The army demands that they will protect all factories and businesses. The military has always coordinated to the states; the new state will remain the same until it is overturned.

The United States has cut multiple millions of American dollars destined in aid to our Mideast ally Egypt. This was in view of the first democratically elected president and the outrageous strength of protesters that has caused a violent turnaround. The State Department aid did not indicate the current amount of dollars this represents, but most of the money is linked to $1.5 billion, which the U.S. gives in aid to Egypt.

Officials state that the aid withheld begins with ten Apache helicopters at $500 million, M-IA one tank assemblies, and Harpoon missiles. Additionally $260 million in cash assistance to the government set up through free and fair elections. The U.S. has provided for F-16 aircraft and has cancelled future US-Egyptian exercises. General Abdel Fattah el Sissi described relations with the U.S. as strategic and founded on similar interest. Israel spoke up, proclaiming that U.S. aid to Egypt is an important link for peace between two countries. The State Department stresses that the long-term relationship between the United States and Egypt is not permanent, yet there is no attempt that President Obama has no interest to end specific programs. The U.S. will support actions that provide support for health, education, counterterrorism, military parts, and odd infinitesimal to keep security at the Siani Peninsula.

The United States of America has been considering such a move since when the Egyptian military replaced Mohammed Morsi. The November trial of Morsi stated he aroused to action to the killings of opponents while in office, and this outcome will depend on the U.S. to cut its aid and will attempt to add to this controversy.

RUSSIA
The Soviet Union (Russia)

Russia remains a Cold War threat and repeatedly challenged us with Putin's tactics. In 2009 a new view of the Soviet Union and its regenerated submarine power made its appearance in August. Two Akula class subs paraded the East Coast of the United States. According to other information, the source was confirmed, but what was the purpose of straddling the Continental Shelf? Two purposes come to mind: Naval Station Norfolk, Virginia; and Kings Bay, Georgia. Kings Bay, Georgia, is a submarine base that was built for eight U.S. nuclear ballistic submarines, the targets of the Akula class. This submarine has a

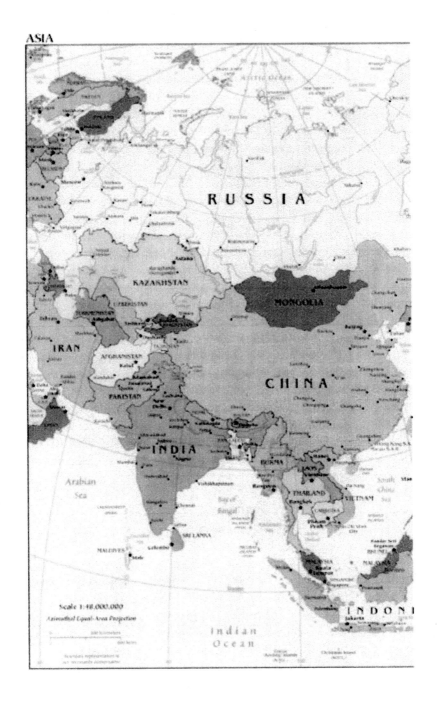

particular large tailfin and is equipped with SSN-21 and SSN-27 launched cruise missiles. This boat can also lay mines.

In 2012 another Russian submarine was detected in the Gulf of Mexico, which until then was undetected by all sources. The second time, it patrolled close to its USA shores. Its stealthy surprise in the Gulf placed when Russian strategic bombers made an unheard of penetrations into U.S. airspace near Alaska and California in June/July 2012. Officials say the unfound defiantly anti-submarine warfare has breached beyond our defense capability. These are detrimental to our security while facing severe cuts while spending reduced amounts in the next ten-year timeframe. According to one official, the Akula operated for almost a month without detection. Since its target is U.S. Navy "boomers," located in Kings Bay, a very stealthy sub can sneak around and avoid detection by any protective screen a ballistic sub can employ. The latest incursion in the Gulf highlights Obama's "reset" policy, which will further relations with Russia.

In June 2012 Russian nuclear bombers conducted a moderate scale simulated attack in the Arctic Ocean. Simulated threats are not always true; the exercise was against the U.S. missile sites in Alaska. This episode was the first since 1991 since the Soviet Union collapsed. In regularity, this is a bold stunt of the Soviets that was designed to further displease to counter U.S. and NATO plans by deploying missile defenses in Europe. In defending the Gulf with clear shallow water, SOSUS acoustic devices, and even satellites can penetrate/detect and track these modern submarines.

On November 5, 2012, another nuclear submarine cruised two hundred miles off the East Coast, similar to the two Akula subs in 2009. The sub was identified as a Russian Sierra 2 Class because of the sensitive nature that bellies the ASW efforts; it pokes around Kings Bay, where our U.S. ballistic and cruise missile submarines are based. An unknown official said the intruder concentrated on staying away from aircraft carrier strike group conducting exercises in the eastern Atlantic. Interesting to note is the Russian AGI ship, or an electronic intelligence gathering data, was permitted to seek shelter in Jacksonville, Florida during a super storm that battered the entire East Coast. The undersea sonar detection devices picked up contact by the Sierra 2 Class sometime late in October.

For the past five years, Russia has but to task numerous acts that have upset the U.S. military and does affect the higher-ups of the White House. In the villa perched on the Elbe River, a major in the Soviet Secret Police recruited people to spy on the West. Vladimir Putin looked for the East Germans, who were professors, scientist, and the like, who could link up with spies permanently assigned in the West. The cold was stealing Western or NATO classified secrets. Such is the background who emerged as a Russian leader.

Putin was picked not by the roll of the dice but by President Boris Yeltsin to become prime minister. He spent seventeen years as a mid-space level agent in the KGB (Komitet Gosudarstvennoi Bezopasnosti), passing by others that were top drawer. Yet Putin witnessed the fall of the finale of the cold war. He fought for not reverting to totalitarianism but maintained a competitive political system.

Putin was born in Leningrad to a farmer and his wife shortly after Stalin's death. He graduated from Stalingrad State University, where his lecturer said his law department was a training ground for the KGB. After a few years of spying on foreigners, he was summoned to Moscow, where he attended an elite foreign institute. He was sent to Germany, where Berlin was an instant source of cold war tensions and machination. The broad "Stasi" network was used by the KGB, which by secret meant it kept Moscow advised.

He returned to St. Petersburg and took a job in a "cover story," and he continued to work for the KGB, spying on students as rector of the university. He had a few rounds with Solchak. After the defeat of Solchak in 1996, Putin left for Moscow with a form, a mining institute, when working with the Kremlin. The title is much to do about the strategic planning of materials and associated raw materials. As reported a newspaper editor requested that he review this piece, but the officials pulled back this document, saying that this was private intelligence. This subject continues on with many quirks becoming a vivacious lie when questioned about the KGB. In a long, laborious talk with Moscow's "Pen Group," the question came up of the KGB role in the Soviet regulation on terror. In response Putin recalls that in 1937, the U.S. did not need a glorified intelligence apprehending us to keep our Soviet Union free from knoss.

In the present time, let's look at the Soviet Union's recent attacks from 2009:

a. Two nuclear attack subs parading the East Coast, August 2009;
b. Two Bear – H strategic bombers' activity near the border, 2011;
c. Activity near Alaskan Air Defense Zone during war games in the Arctic in late June 2011;
d. A harder-to-detect Akula in the Gulf of Mexico in August 2012;
e. A Sierra Two Class Submarine made the exact pass skirting the Continental Shelf, November 2012.
f. Norway's military reported a Bear/Bomber on September 11 and 12, 2012, followed by NATO jet fighters.

The instantaneous steps verify that the cold war continues! From a USA perspective, the Russians are interested in oil, pure and simple. They have been talking to Canada since our leader has kept the question of the Keystone pipeline. On again and off, this dilemma is ripe for the Russians to secure. Let's look at what the Gepard Akula II found at this underhanded adventure into the Gulf of Mexico. The Northern Fleet reports the mission of the submarine was not one of power but of economics that weights buying BP's Gulf of Oil asset, for which they are asking $7.9 billion. The total amount of oil leaking into the water was five thousand barrels a day, when the real amount of twenty-five thousand barrels per day led to the largest cover-up in U.S. history.

As the highest intelligence leader of the Russian government, he relies on his background, the conniving supercilious and with full knowledge of the background of the KGB, Putin will succeed in all details! Through him all facets of all particular countries are being superseded in treaties that restore military technical support of the ships, plus special benefits. Cam Ranh Bay, Vietnam, Lourdes, Cuba, and Seychelles in the Indian Ocean are primary areas, and such are necessary by our loved land of freedom. Another tidbit of info: Venezuela will get eleven submarines, including a new Akula attack submarine. Venezuela is rapidly building up its forces with planes and weaponry. Does this factor cause chimes to ring in the United States Defense Department?

We are pondering over our weak economy dragging us down, and the president being intimated by Putin, not taking well to not having his way in any given situation.

CHAPTER 4

OBAMACARE

In 2006, according to the United States Census Bureau, about 60% of all Americans obtained their health insurance coverage through their employers. Another 9% purchased their health insurance directly. About 16% were covered under various government-sponsored plans, such as Medicare or the Veterans Health Administration. The remaining 15% were uninsured. Of those uninsured, it is estimated that at least half of them could have obtained affordable coverage but chose not to do so. Many young people in their twenties and early thirties see themselves as invincible. The prospect of injury, illness, or disease seems remote. So why spend what little money they have on something as boring as health insurance? Most would rather spend their money on a new car, new clothes, the latest iPhone, or a premium TV package than make the modest financial sacrifice required to assure the quality of their healthcare by purchasing health insurance. Therefore, it is with little wonder that much of young America fell under the spell of Barack Obama when he promised them free subsidized or affordable healthcare. This is a promise that he has not kept. Obama's healthcare plan is a disaster and one our nation cannot afford!

Life expectancy in the United States is 78.4 years at birth, ranking 50th among 220 nations. Of the 17 highest-income nations, the National Institute of Health reported in 2012 that the USA has some of the highest rates of infant mortality, heart disease, sexually transmitted infections, adolescent pregnancies, homicides, and commonplace disabilities—all of this in a country that has some of the best doctors and hospitals in the world. Many have concluded that the lack of access to affordable healthcare must be the cause behind our lagging health statistics. After all, the USA is one of the few industrialized countries that does not guarantee access to healthcare for its population! That all changed on March 23, 2010, when the Patient

Protection and Affordable Act was adopted by law, introducing massive changes to America's healthcare system.

A popular Democratic governor from Kansas, Kathleen Sebelius, won the pick as Obama's choice for Health & Human Resources (HHS) Secretary in February 2009. Sebelius is a professional politician who comes from a political party with roots deep in Democratic tradition. Her father is a former Democratic governor of Ohio. Sebelius started her political career in 1986, when she was elected to the Kansas House of Representatives. She later went on to become the Insurance Commissioner of Kansas, and she held this position for eight years. Apparently, this is where she developed the skills and qualifications that Obama felt worthy of his choice for HHS Secretary. It would be her job to create and launch Obama's vision of building a new health program. As HHS Secretary, she was a key player in the massive overhaul of the American healthcare system.

During her first month in the Obama Administration, Sebelius debated formerly for healthcare reform. Her attitude toward the problem was that the current government plan wasn't worth reforming. The approach adopted was for mandatory insurance coverage, which both houses passed on March 21, 2010. This process was known as the reconciliation, where the lower house with a simple majority passed the amendment. The $94-billion bill, known as the Patient Protection and Affordable Care Act or (PPACA), aka "Obamacare," became law and requires all Americans to purchase health insurance, plus requires insurance companies to cover them. Since the president signed Obamacare into law, the Office of Management & Budget now estimates the cost to be over $2 trillion. This is no misprint—that is twelve zeroes. Two trillion dollars! Or put another way, over $6,000 for every man, woman, and child in the United States. And all of this for the benefit for less than 10% of all Americans who do not have health insurance, many who can afford it but choose not to purchase it.

So how does the healthcare law protect our citizens in getting new affordable health insurance? The Obama Plan can—or can it? The two thousand pages of the bill were not read or fully understood by our representatives in Congress or the American people before it was passed into law. We now know the bill contains restrictions and hidden costs, fees, and fines that are creating uncertainty of the minds of the business community and prolonging the economic recession that should have ended long ago. Obama has broken his promises. The Affordable Care Act is not affordable. Many are having to pay more, and many are finding their coverage unsatisfactory. If you believe in this fairytale of Obamacare, forget it and read on.

The PPACA is just a new way for all persons to get a bonafide insurance by turning individual responsibility over to the government. Insurance companies will no longer be allowed to apply underwriting standards to applicants for coverage and must accept all who apply, regardless of any preexisting conditions that one may have. This approach penalizes the healthy and forces subsidizing the unhealthy through higher premiums. In addition, some healthy individuals who prefer minimal health plans are now finding their coverage is being cancelled because it doesn't meet the minimum mandated federal standards. But Obama promised you could keep your doctors and keep your current insurance. Another broken promise, or an outright lie? The danger in Obamacare is that once the federal government takes control of our healthcare system, they will determine who gets treated, how they are treated, and where they are treated. The ultimate cost will become so staggering that they will begin to ration care and mandate doctors' fees, just as they do with Medicare today. And as anyone on Medicare will tell you, some of the best doctors do not accept Medicare patients because they can't afford to treat them for what the government pays them for their services. The result will be fewer people entering the medical profession and more doctors leaving the medical profession, and at the same time more people insured under the PPACA will be seeking treatment. In short, once the government starts telling doctors what they can charge, doctors will start leaving the medical profession, resulting in too few doctors, rationing of service, and lower quality of medical care for all of us.

"Spinning out of control" was the saying about the propensity of Obamacare. Republicans, as well as those Democrats against the creation of all things great and expensive, believe that they should join hands and sabotage this act. As one man said, "It's like throwing hand grenades, which are spearheaded by all Republican leaders of both the House and Senate." The Affordable Care Act should be repealed.

Twenty-one governors have opted out of a medical explosion and have refused to set up an insurance plan. Obamacare will expand to fewer Americans as a result of a direct bypass and Republican resistance. Also, the law's complete and unbelievable implosion when it debuts during 2014. Senators are mincing premiums that will catapult while ads claim that they will lose access to their doctors. State officials are worried that this program is being set up on the ground; however, they cringe when the Creator speaks. On October 1, 2013, they will comparison shop, like buying TVs or airline tickets. Local and State officials think that health insurance will be easier to access than before. With all of the bumps and misinformation, it will take longer than buying a high-priced item from Best Buy. Being not available for a specific program, they might need to spend additional ideas on the phone hashing all the parameters of a particular circuliam. When buying a plane ticket, one does not enter a social security number, an annual income, or other such data.

The Associated Press owned up to an eternal government document, which showed Obama's officials were, in fact, concerned about the *Healthcare.gov* website dated Sept 27, 2003, which was three days prior to the rollout. This friend of the Press is concerned that universal healthcare is slowly staggering, which showed how little they care about you and how totally incompetent the government is.

This incompetence is John McCain's priority, down to destroying both Mike Lee and Tom Cruz. Evidently Medicare Chief Marilyn Tavenner was able to test different facets in security in one version of this program. This, no joke, is one of Marilyn's thrown under the bus.

President Obama unexpectedly delayed a vital key in the Affordable Care Act in pursuit of sedating the calm among the public and the near miss of revolt of the Democratic Party. Even through his missteps that exploded into trouble, he announced that insurance companies would be granted approval to renew for a year health plans that fail to meet the new law standards. At stake was his "mega gulps" new conference in the White House that was planted at doing a one hundred-eighty-degree turnaround, a falling slide that would put him in peril, which could threaten his term as president.

After three years of haggling, the Republicans have had little success fighting the Affordable Care Act. This was based on the first six weeks of the botched rollout of the Federal Exchange website, plus broken promises when consumers were able to keep insurance plans that have fallen in decay and torn down Obama's writing on the wall which, of course, the Democrats backed most high! The president had not been told of the rocky road that this website will endure. He apologized for the fumbled snake policy of this rollout and insisted that this slapped around a computer glitch that would be fixed.

Another backslap was noted when changing of the rules at such a late date would probably disable the market and look out for rising premiums! In other words, the changes as invoked by the president cannot be put in a situation where a change cannot be put into effect. House Republicans plan to vote on a bill and the White House opposes this enactment that Americans will keep their previous medical plan until 2014. Mary Landrieu of Louisiana signaled that they plan to move ahead with a proposal that ensures it would make their plans permanent. This and other discrepancies of this defunct plan is, according to the Brookins Institute, a hurricane of trouble when looking at 39% to 52% approval rating. This, of course, is representative that President Obama is not a strong and capable leader. Thus, the Obama prospect is boulders of granite puncturing the earth and when a reporter asked him about

Iran's nuclear power, it must have been a diversion. Americans who have been committed to this outrageous healthcare debate are blaming the president for raising premiums and deductibles, and overall 75% say the rollout for the uninsured falls lower and lower. Keeping the healthcare program from falling into evil days is his spot-on challenge. The Brookings Poll found 85% of Americans don't have to be worried about this issue. These people will have to worry about their changing policies that will take them to 2014. Nearly four out of five represent a dislike of the Affordable Care Act even though the trend toward leaner coverage predicts the present law passed.

Rightfully or wrongly, the persons signing up with private insurance are nervous about what is really going to happen. Care documentation will prevail among the American people in 2014. Disapproval of Obama's plan copped an average of 60% in this poll. The Democrats are hoping that the evildoers will fade in their minds. Poll wise, the Donkeys were 32% versus the Elephants when it comes to who should control healthcare. Recently the poll taken shows 11% of Americans said that someone in their household tried to sign up for health coverage in the new marketplaces. In total 12% in their household plans ran into problems. About one-fourth managed to enroll and have said they cannot purchase insurance, and the remaining fourth said they were not sure of buying new contracts.

Many people are in a quandary over Obamacare, especially since most other proposals offered better options and solutions than the Obama plan. One such proposal offers a simple approach; it starts with the same basic premise that healthcare is a basic need. At some point in all of our lives, we will need a doctor. In a compassionate society, healthcare should be accessible to all. However, the reality is someone has to pay for it, and no one wants to subsidize healthcare insurance for someone who can pay for it themselves.

The simple plan works like this:

1. No free healthcare: Doctors, hospitals, labs, and pharmaceutical companies all have a right to get paid and to make a fair profit. If an individual requires medical services, they are expected to have health insurance. If we don't allow our healthcare providers to prosper and reap the benefits of their long and expensive educations, we will inevitably experience shortages of doctors and a general decline in the quality of our healthcare.

2. Mandatory health insurance coverage for all. Anyone without health insurance will be automatically enrolled, on the spot, by the medical

provider into an assigned government-sponsored private health insurance plan. This plan must accept anyone, and premiums are simply based on the age of the individual. As a result, this plan will not be in the cheapest and individuals in this plan will be motivated to find cheaper coverage in the private marketplace.

3. The government-sponsored private plan. This is basically an exchange where private health insurance companies contract with the government to provide this coverage. Yes, the premiums will be higher, but everyone will have access to coverage and to the same medical providers as individuals who seek out and purchase their own health insurance in the private marketplace.

4. Rewards and incentives. Once in this assigned plan, the only way out is to provide proof that coverage has been secured elsewhere. The first year in the plan, the uninsured are accessed a 10% penalty for not having purchased private coverage as required. Remember, these people would not even be in the plan if they had not been uninsured and needed medical care. If they remain in the plan, they will begin to earn credits for each year their medical expenses are below a certain standard. This will motivate some healthy individuals to stay in the plan, whereby driving down the cost for everyone in the plan. It will also act as an incentive to seek preventative care and to live a healthy lifestyle. In addition, the deductable options will allow individuals to assume greater risks for their own healthcare costs.

5. Cost and subsidies. How do we pay for this? Everyone who can is expected for their own health insurance. After all, the government doesn't subsidize individuals' auto insurance or life insurance. This may mean that some folks will have to make sacrifices to foot the bill. But if we truly believe that healthcare is an important basic need, shouldn't we demand our fellow citizens exercise some basic personal financial responsibilities for their own healthcare? How many people driving new cars don't have health insurance? How many college students chatting away on iPhones don't have health insurance? The "government" can't pay for your healthcare unless you are willing to surrender your freedoms (and tax dollars) to it. Beware of the government that controls your healthcare, for it will soon control every aspect of your life!

For all, healthcare expenses and premiums should be tax deductable. This will help ease the burden of health insurance for many. For the truly poor, disabled, sick, and needy who cannot afford anything, a compassionate society picks up the tab. None of us would trade places with the sick or poor, but we can have the satisfaction of knowing they have access to healthcare. However, if their circumstances should change, we should also expect some level of reimbursement for prior subsidies. There is no free ride for those who can afford to pay.

Benefits to this plan:

- Everyone has access to the same quality of care.
- Individuals with existing conditions are not discriminated against.
- Each age group has a rate reflective of the cost for their age.
- No distinction made between men and women.
- Subsidized individuals will pay as much as they can afford.
- Incentives exist for subsidized individuals to move to the private pay plan when they can afford it.
- Costs for this plan are covered by premiums and premium tax. It can never run out of money and doesn't require any money from the government other than the premium tax they collect from the people. Administrative costs are covered by the insurance companies.

What is the answer? Not Obamacare! We can do much better. But it is no secret that Obama does not really care about the quality of your healthcare. He has long advocated for a government single-pay system that will put all of your healthcare decisions in the hands of a government bureaucrat. Next time you are standing in line at the U.S. Post Office, imagine what your healthcare could be like under a government-run healthcare system.

Website glitches will be long forgotten on the next election day. At least that's what a lot of Democrats hope. Why are some Democrats seething over the polls present day or what has happened to the ownership of the healthcare law? President Obama has dropped another bomb concerning people with a plan that have gained insurance. Senate Majority Harry Reid said his Democratic team will prove Obamacare to be a positive goal for the Democratic candidates in 2014.

The Federal Government asks insurers to extend people extra time to purchase health insurance by January 1, 2014, even though this is not what the law requires. HHS Kathleen Sebelius said people would have extra time to sign up by December 23 for the January 1 coverage. The changes initiated by Sebelius are aimed at filling the holes for buying insurance through Federal and State exchanges. The problem is October 1 has been plagued by rollout discrepancies declared fixed November 1, 2013.

On April 1, 2014, the news of today is triumphantly announced that President Obama has 7.1 million Americans who have selected Obamacare. The total is in question, as many have signed up for private insurance through these marketplaces. Why is it that many people, like Republicans and conservatives, strike their actions on Obamacare disapproval? Social Security is going bankrupt (the former secretary of treasury) said the opposite when he lied about Social Security, and he has the power of government to supply the action. The real reason the number of people don't sign up is because of the restrictions on insurance and reimbursement rates to doctors.

These are the preliminary stats that will indicate between 2% and 5% paid their January 2014 bill, but not so in February. The 7.1 million people are not important, but Obama will manufacture his numbers by hook or by crook.

The bottom line is that Obamacare is an abomination for the American people. The law was shoved down our throats with no real debate or bipartisan support. The costs were deliberately underestimated, and it is now proving to be unaffordable for our country. The administration of the rollout has been disastrous. But what else should we have expected from our federal government?

The Affordable Act is law. Frankly, there are some good components to it. However, in whole is restraining from the rebound we urgently need. It may not be possible to repeal the law in its entirety, but a major overhaul is possible and necessary if we are to move forward as a country. Obama's handling of his hallmark redistribution legislative achievement has divided the country. It is time for America to fix this law and advance. This can only happen if more like-minded individuals are elected to Congress and the White House. If this is to happen, the Republicans will need to present a precise plan for change that is consistent with conservative ideals and budget considerations.

CHAPTER 5

BENGHAZI ATTACK, 2012

America will soon have to believe that there is a scandal covering all the bullshit that the Obama Administration had been talking behind closed doors about the Benghazi interaction and its unfumbling aftermath. The White House and State Department orchestrated by Hillary Clinton knew well that the Benghazi encounter was inspired by the al Qaeda right from the get-go. Drawing from the start, there is new evidence that they were expecting this attack for several months. According to one individual, we have one decision: Leave Benghazi or you will be killed. Lieutenant Colonel Andy Wood was a top-secret man who met with Ambassador Stevens every day. In June, the months before the attack, al Qaeda tried to assassinate the British ambassador. Wood said the attack came as no surprise to him. With online posters, the al Qaeda were saying that they would attack the Red Cross, the British, and the Americans in Benghazi. As they attacked Red Cross and the British mission, they antagonized each other and they realized it was going to happen. We included our reports to both the State Department and the Department of Defense. Andy Wood informed Ambassador Stevens three months before the compound was overrun!

Andy Wood made it clear that you are going to be attacked, and you need a change in your security profile. Basically your operation should change locations within the city. Be flexible and the terrorists are keeping an eagle eye on you. The final attack can be verifiable depending on this facility.

Abu Anas al Libi was known by the United States, and he was working with others to establish a secret terrorist organization within this country. Al Libi was wanted for his role in the bombing of two United States Embassies in Africa.

In view of the criticality of things belonging to the night in Libya, my trust is that Secretary Clinton and President Obama had all of the intelligence warning them of an attack in Benghazi. This repartee is not only the whistle-blowers who are talking about such an attack in Benghazi. Gregory Hicks gave similarly damaging testimony to Congress, but the grandfather White House continued to turn the other eye and obfuscate any attempts to gain the truth.

We continue to plead to representatives of Congress for answers about the murders of American citizens overseas. The complexity of President Obama and Secretary Clinton in the deaths and cover-ups of these four Americans deserves the exact reason of death rather than forgetting what happened or saying, "What does it matter?" about what happened in Libya in 2012.

The American Diplomatic in Benghazi in Libya was attacked on September 11, 2012. The attack, which was reported as heavily armed groups, began at night and was to protect the consulate building. A second assault occurred early in the morning under attack and was a nearby Central Intelligence Agency Annex in a different part of the Diplomatic Compound. Four people were killed: U.S. Ambassador J. Christopher Stevens, Diplomat Sean Smith, Tyrone Woods, and Glen Doherty. The other members of the consulate were injured. In all due respect, this was strongly condemned by the governments of Libya, the United States, and the list of countries grows throughout the world.

Libyans noted with great administration of the ambassadors and weighed a strong displeasure of the groups that formed during a civil war against Colonel Gaddafi. The United States is seeking an answer to the four slain members of this bug-a-boo scenario and involves a series of episodes that determines who is responsible for this heinous act. Initially, there was speculation who to a medicated attack by Islamic militants. Finally, the Republican Party of the U.S. accused the President of the United States and the Secretary of State, Hillary Clinton, as withholding pertinent data regarding this event.

BACKGROUND

In the aftermath of this crisis, integrated noted a dozen events in Benghazi during the past six months. Republicans Darrell Issa and Jason Chaffetz, plus Homeland Security and others, sent a letter to the Secretary of State, Clinton, which listed each event. Clearly the information was never followed through, which described the deficiencies that needed to be connected post haste!

In April 2012, two former guards threw a "fish bomb" instant explosive device "IED" over the consulate fence. Just four days later, a similar bomb was thrown at the United Nations Special Envoy, which suffered no injuries.

In May 2012 the al Qaeda affiliate broadcasted the Imperial Oural Aubul Rahman Budaces (IOARB). It was responsible for a raid on the Red Cross office in Benghazi. The Red Cross was outraged by the incident and was concerned about the increasing violence in Libya.

IOARB released a video that said it had detonated an explosive outside the U.S. gates on June 5. The Brigades offered that the attack was in response to the killing of Abu Yahya Al Libii, who had died in a U.S. drone attack.

The British Ambassador to Libya survived an assassination attempt on July 10, where two men were injured. The British withdrew their consulate staff from Benghazi by the end of June.

On June 18, 2012, the Tunisian consulate was stormed by individuals who were associated with Ansar Al-Sharia Lybia.

On September 11, 2008, al Qaeda leader Ayman Al Zauahiri declared Libya's death must be avenged.

Egypt reports two thousand Salatists actively protested against the film *Innocence of Muslims* at the U.S. Embassy in Cairo. President Obama attended a 9/11 ceremony and later visited Walter Reed National Military Medical Center for two or three men who had been injured at the beginning Benghazi attack.

In Benghazi a plan for gunrunning was in the apparent scheme to aid the Syrian rebels. Washington, D.C., and President Obama were involved in it and were headed by an unknown Muslim Brotherhood from Dallas, Texas.

Ambassador Stevens was in Benghazi to deal with the Obama Administration to arm Syrian rebels. Through shipping records of "The Victory," the Libyan-flagged vessel *Al Entisal* was received in the Turkish port of Iskenderun about thirty-four miles from Syria on September 6, 2012. This data was only five days before the ambassador plus three men were decimated during an assault of over one hundred Islamic terrorists.

On the night of September 1, 2012, Stevens met with Turkish Consul General Ali Sali Akin, who escorted him out at one hour before the skirmish started at the consulate. According to sources, the meeting was to sell the arrangement of the deadly SA-7—portable SAMs—to Islamists and other al Qaeda, the Assad regime in Syria. Obama had a friendly relationship with the Turkish Prime Minister Recep Tayyip Erdogan, and the alliance was discouraged with Islamists in Syria battling Assad in the exchange before. In other brief remarks, Ambassador Stevens was facilitating weapons transfers from Libya to Syria Islamic forces coordinated with Al Qaeda via his Turkish association. We are courting danger, if not, great disaster in this public history! We have been at war with the Islamic hydra with al Qaeda for a decade, yet known sources are accessible accusing a president of resting on his bullocks! Providing munitions to al-Qaeda-aligned Islamic forces would meet the treason, which has so been stranded. The Obama Administration has violated this charge to which it must answer and should be offered no quarter!

Two security guards noticed a Libyan policeman taking pictures of the consultant talking on his cell phone. These guards briefly detained the man, and he drove off in the police car. Sean Smith noticed the whole episode and posted it on the internet: "Assuming we will not die tonight, we saw one of our policemen who guard the compound taking pictures."

THE ATTACK

File:U.S. mission and annex map for 2012 Benghazi attack.jpg

From Wikipedia, the free encyclopedia

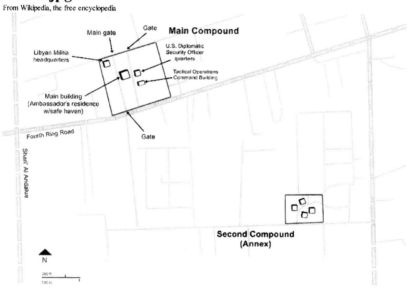

Map of the United States mission (main compound) and annex.

The Benghazi attack consisted of two military factions on two separate United States compounds. The main enclosed facility, which is three hundred yards logged and approximately one hundred yards wide, was attacked about 9:40 P.M. local time or 3:40 P.M. EDT. The second barrage took place at the CIA Annex, which is 1.2 miles away or about 4:00 A.M. local time the next day.

Between one hundred twenty-five and one hundred fifty men wearing the Afghan-style tunics favored by the Islamic militants were reported in the assault. Their faces were covered and they wore flak shirts. Weapons that were used were rocket-propelled grenades (RPG's), AK-47 rifles, assault rifles, mortars, heavy machine guns, and artillery mounted on trucks. The attack began at midnight with the ceiling off starts leading to the main compound. The truck bore the logo of Asar Al Sharia, which tended to lend support with the Islamic supporters who tried to maintain security in Benghazi.

Outside the establishment before the battle, the assault was quiet. Passing by the lawyer, he saw twenty youths. There were no more than seven Americans, including Ambassador Stevens, who was visiting Benghazi to review plans to establish a new cultural center and to reorganize a hospital. The ambassador had concluded his meeting with a Turkish diplomat and was safely in quarters at 8:30 P.M. Ambassador Stevens retired at 9:00 P.M. according to guards interviewed after the fracas.

At 9:40 P.M., the sound "Allahu Akbar" descended on the compound led by large numbers of men and grenades, and men entered the building, along with automatic rifle fire, RPG's, and truck-mounted firepower. A diplomatic Security Service viewed this on the security cameras; he hit the alarm, shouting, "Attack, attack!" over the loud speaker. Phone calls were made to the embassy in Tripoli; the Diplomatic Security Compound Center in Washington, D.C.; the Libyan Brigade; and the U.S. Quick Reaction Force, located one mile away. Ambassador Stevens telephoned Deputy Chief of Mission Gregory Hicks in Tripoli that the consulate was under attack. Mr. Hicks did not recognize the phone ringing; however, he answered it on the last ring.

Deputy Security Service Special Agent Strickland secured Ambassador Stevens and Sean Smith in the main complex safe haven. Other agents received their M-4 carbines and tactical gear from another building. They tried to reach the three persons but encountered armed men and then retreated. The Strike Force entered the main building and knocked the metal grille of this safe haven. They carried jerry cans of diesel fuel and spread it over chairs and the floor, and set fires. As smoke filled the building, U.S. personnel moved to the basement and lay on the floor. Being overcome by smoke, Strickland exited through the window, but Stevens and Smith did not follow him. Strickland went up to the roof and radioed other agents. Three men in an armed vehicle went to the safe haven and found Smith's body, but not Stevens'.

The Regional Security Office sounded the alarm. Benghazi CIA Annex and the embassy said, "We are under attack and we need help." Tyrone Woods decided a rescue was needed, so at 10:05 P.M. the team was briefed and armored Toyota Land Cruisers were launched. Another CIA element was trying to get to the compound, which included Glen Doherty. The team arrived at the site and attempted to secure the perimeter. They found Smith, unconscious, and later declared him dead. An all-hands effort, they could not find the ambassador. Quickly the team moved back to the annex, but while halfway back to the final destination, they were hit by AK-47's and grenades. The vehicle was able to make the annex with two flat tires, and the gates closed behind them at 11:50 P.M. According to Libya's Supreme Security Committee, all roads were sealed off with Security Forces surrounding it.

The Benghazi situation depends on a signal factor: granting or withholding "cross-border authority" (CBA). Once the gong of the clock is set from the consulate in Benghazi, dozens of headquarters are notified and are planning in real time. This alert includes AFICOM and EURCOM, located in Germany. They can plan to move troops and forces, ships, and aircraft, forward to the location of crisis. Without explicit orders from the president, you can't cross international borders on a hostile mission! "Red Line" is a clear type of a crisis scenario. No administration wanted to barrage into war because a jet jockey strays into hostile territory. Only the President of the United States (POTUS) can authorize our military to cross a nation's border without that nation's permission. The other side of the coin: In order to prevent military action in Benghazi, the POTUS has to grant CBA authority. Ships can loiter on station, aircraft can fall out of the blue, so they must be directed to an air base to await POTUS on granting CBA. If the decision is not to invoke CBA, the assets are dependent on Benghazi or quick-action forces including the independent Predator Drones. Assets could be moved or placed as the acting ambassadors or CIA station chief in Libya.

Diplomatic Security Service Agent / Regional Security Officers informed Washington, D.C., that at 9:40 (3:40 P.M. eastern time), the attack had begun. Let's turn to the White House and its 4:30 P.M. conducting a meeting with Defense Secretary Panetta , POTUS, and the VPOTUS. In the words of the president, "I think we should not go the military route." Case closed? By 4:30 P.M., the Pentagon directives informed Secretary of Defense Leon Panetta of the attack, where a drone was dispatched to the area at 5:11 P.M. and provided a live video feed to Washington, D.C. They shut down all efforts to help them and ended their lives, Ambassador Stevens and three others. Their "standing orders" now go down the chain of command—to Secretary of Defense General Dempsey to General Ham, plus other commanders who are gearing up plans to rescue these besieged consulate. The POTUS apparently thought the battle was over, so he went upstairs to his family quarters, or maybe he made himself unavailable! His standing order prevails until the next morning, September 12, 2012. Nobody in the military or otherwise below POTUS can overturn his ability to send troops in Libyan air space. Not even Panetta, Hillary Clinton, not General Dempsey, and not even General Ham in Stuttgart, Germany, who is in charge of all staging in Sigonella, Sicily. In essence, we don't know where the president was hour by hour! This is 100 % true: Panetta and Dempsey should have commented a rescue mission if the president had given these orders.

The CIA, Department of Naval Intelligence (DNI), and the Pentagon watched with a feeble plea of no response. Once the attack commenced, 10:00 P.M. or 4:00 P.M. EST, the mission security staff immediately contacted Washington and our embassy in Tripoli. The White House, including all branches of diplomacy/intelligence forces, watched an overhead drove, and cries for help/assistance went unanswered.

Four hundred miles from the assault is Sigonella, Sicily, where a fully equipped Special Forces with both transport and jet aircraft were positioned. His local commander at Sigonella was ready to launch; however, this was countermanded—who is responsible? He must be high in the administration to make such a callous decision. No one at the CIA told anybody not to help these under attack. Was the director of the CIA and head of National Intelligence in deep kaimshe over the fabrication and cover-up?

The executive orders have to be realized according to General Ham. This is why cross-border authority is the King Arthur's Sword in understanding the debacle of Benghazi. Only POTUS and only he can extract forcibly that sword. No general or admiral will hang on the line when advancing ahead on undertaking a mission gone wrong that the president later denies. This rule of instruction yet claims it's a "loose cannon" or "rouge commands" blowing their responsibility. Panella or General Dempsey, with subject compliance to silence, how far does loyalty and esprit de corps last when covering gross neglect of duty by the President of the United States? At 5:41 P.M., Secretary of State Hillary Clinton telephoned CIA Director David Petraeus. General Petraeus was stepping carefully with his ridiculous on his fare, however, early in the cover-up with the CIA intelligence link, and now he felt burned. By an agreement reached in early 2012, the arms were taken from Gaddafi's arsenals and moved to Syria. David Petraeus, the CIA director, ran the operation. He admits that the stand-down did not come from the CIA. The CIA is only outranked by the National Security Team at the White House. This means President Obama and he is naming him without question, not he himself! This without a granite boulder striking water, this is better than blowing a whistle—better than the horrific status of a general and the Secretary of Defense. CIA had long believed that a ten-member security strike force would assist in the event of an assault.

42

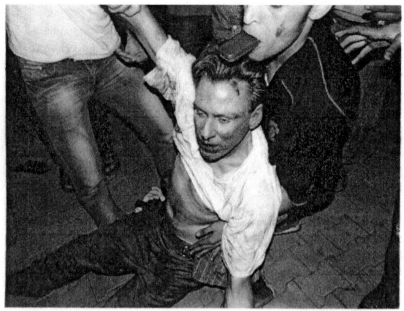

Libyan allies try in vain to save unconscious, victim of fiery attack believed to be terrorist plot.

U.S. Ambassador Stevens found dead during the attack.

At 1:00 A.M., the body of Ambassador Stevens was found by local residents and his body was taken to Benghazi Medical Center. He was given cardiopulmonary resuscitation (CPR) for ninety minutes, and according Dr. Ziad Abu Zeid he died from asphyxiation with massive smoke in a small room. This, among other things, proved the U.S. Ambassador died after the building was set on fire. Some of the Libyans found Stevens lying in the dark smoke-filled room with a locked door accessible only by a window. Several men moved him outside on the courtyard tiled floor. At the hospital, Dr. Zeid said the officers from the Libyans' interior ministry transported the body to the airport, where the U.S. took custody.

The attack on the CIA annex began shortly after midnight, which included machinegun and mortar fire. The intensive fire lasted until morning September 12, 2012. A Libyan enforcement group of Americans included Glen Doherty and met at the Benghazi Airport. The Libyan forces/American actives were built up for a few hours. After activities were held up for a few hours and at 5 A.M., they went to the CIA Compound to get thirty-two Americans and began evacuation to the airport. As they were passing through the gates, the annex came under heavy fire. After a lull in the firing, Glen Doherty began to search for his buddy Tyrone Woods. He found him on the roof manning a MK-46 machinegun. They quickly embraced and started to retake the defensive firing. Soon Woods was taken out with a mortar, virtually wounding him. As Doherty attempted to change from one position to another, a second round fell on him, killing him instantly. Immediately several men climbed the roof and damage and helped the men. At the same time, a JSDC operator was analyzing the data displaying images from a predator drone, which was sent by the DOD African Command after CIA request. This told them they had better start moving toward the airport as a large mass was assembling. Within minutes all vehicles were loaded and they were en route to the airfield. On the way, they were hit by gunfire and no further injuries were obtained. At 3:40 P.M. (9:40 P.M. Benghazi time), Washington intelligence was notified of the attack on the Benghazi mission. This broad band of communication enabled all units, including the White House as well as the Pentagon, FBI, and other governmental agencies.

THE WHITE HOUSE

Unclassified and unbeknown to spies are the photos that were posted two days ago of the Oval Office, September 11, 2012. This graphic reveals a picture worth a thousand words! The sunlight provides more than epics can surmise involving the events of Benghazi, Libya. During this attack, worldly efficient men turn the tables over this horrific event.

Denis McDonough, Deputy National Security Advisor, updates the president and vice president on the condition in the Middle East and in North Africa. This picture was taken at 7:28 P.M. D.C. time. It was dusk outside as the president had just finished a call with Prime Minister Benjamin Netanyahu. The importance of this phone call was that it lasted almost an hour! The importance of this phone call was to discuss the threat of Iran's nuclear program and other steps that we should act jointly with other security diplomacy. In other words, this call started three hours after the attack began at 3:40 P.M. D.C. time. It might appear odd to have the president and vice president to be tied up. What are the odds of what could happen needing one immediately? Maybe the hand notes hold the answer. Either Netanyahu or Obama knew Biden was monitoring the phone specifically. The call took place from 12:30 P.M. and 1:26 A.M. Benghazi time.

According to numerous reports, CIA and former Seals Tyrone Woods and Glen Doherty returned from the consulate to the CIA Annex with the body of State Department to Ambassador Steven Sean Smith, without certainty that Ambassador Stevens was missing. During this Oval Office call,

Woods and Doherty were on the roof of the CIA Building, pleading for more support. So was the President of the United States and the vice president not in the command decision loop? Who is making decisions on behalf of the commander-in-chief?

Lindsay showed skill and ingenuity when he was examining Secretary of Defense (Leon Panetta) and General Martin Dempsey. The headline was: President Barack Obama never bothered to contact the chair of the Joint Chiefs of Staff and Secretary of Defense after being informed that the American consulate was under attack by terrorists. The Secretary of Defense had a drone on the area on September 11 and you, the president and the vice president, met in the Oval Office at 5:00 P.M. This was more than an hour after the hostile attack. These fifty minutes of the assault were sent flowing into the Situation Room in the White House. Note: The president missed the daily intelligence briefing for at least five days leading to the September 11, 2012, invasion of the United States Consulate in Benghazi.

At 5:00 EST, first ahead was Defense Secretary Panetta, Chairman of Joint Chiefs Dempsey. White House National Security Advisor Tom Dolion tells POTUS of the attack and fire at the main villa. At 6:07 P.M., an alert from the State Department claims that the U.S. Embassy in Tripoli that an Islamic group, "Asarn al Sharia," claims the attack on Facebook and Twitter and has called for an attack on the embassy Tripoli. The Pentagon orders a Special Operation Team to move Europe and to move to eventually to Sigonella, Sicily, at 6:30 P.M. Who is in charge—POTUS and the vice president, and now back on the phone to Netanyahu! Who's in charge? At 7:30 EST, the first of two unmanned Predator Drones were flying in Eastern Libya and were diverted to Benghazi. Obama and Biden are still on the phone with Netanyahu! At 7:30 P.M. EST, a U.S. Security team lands from the embassy in Tripoli and learns that the ambassador is missing. Representing the commander-in-chief during this critical timeframe is not in compliance at this time.

One of Obama's closet advisors is Deputy National Security Advisor Denis McDonough. He enjoys a well-spaced educated forty-one-year-old, which has limited experience work on the hill and transferring to a think tank Obama gave him that position. McDonough is not good for this position, but embarrassing to the position he now holds. McDonough has a social position around D.C.; he has a rabid mind in his mission to set the record straight. He riles at people talking about being promoted out of step, and he'd like to piss vinegar all over you! Yes, it's too experienced to wash off the verbal piss—it's way too inexperienced.

Tom Donilon told people to "stand down" while POTUS and VP were on the phone with Netanyahu. At 7:26 P.M. EST or 1:30 A.M. Benghazi time, when this picture was taken, Ty Woods and Glen Doherty were sacrificing their lives to defend our country! Neither they nor the great commander-in-chief reversed the call. Perhaps it was too late when at 7:26 P.M. the update was made known of Ambassador Stevens as "missing, presumed dead." This action was initiated by Dennis McDonough to provide a good cover released to the Press.

The hidden story had already existed the same day the State Department was commenting on the attack in Cairo, Egypt. The following was effective on September 12, 2012: "This work takes on added urgency given the truly abhorrent video that has offended so many people, Muslims and non-Muslims alike, in our country and around the world." After all, it was this "kid" who was the deflector between POTUS and the crisis that reflected the "Fast & Furious." His "work" led to many silencing complaints from the CIA. Another thousand words! Another onion to peel, especially the skill by Lindsay Graham upon his investigation of Leon Panetta and General Dempsey. The best and the most: The president never contacted the joint chiefs and the secretary of defense after realizing that an American consulate was under attack. The amount of damaging statements, such as, not one aircraft was launched during the attack, not one boot left the ground outside Libya. About 281 threat reports offered them any indication that Benghazi was designated a high-priority item. Also, Graham asked how many cables came from U.S. Ambassadors stating specifically (as Stevens did) that an American installation could not stand against a sustained attack and government buildings are flying al Qaeda flags. Dempsey tries to pass this on to the State Department; however, Graham injects that Hillary Clinton never did see the cable, which Dempsey clearly had which he submits "it is surprising."

Hearing from Defense Secretary Panetta, we did not send rescue forces because Benghazi did not know the status of the terrorist raid! That statement is valid because there is no real time about the Middle East. Also, there were fifty minutes of real time data of the attack sent screaming into the Situation Room in the White House. Prior to an hour before President Obama and VP Biden, "nobody told us" in the Oval Office before the initial attack.

In the Situation Room, real time data detailing the armed terrorists was attacking our consulate. Ambassador Stevens was crouched in a safe room, yet it indeed bolded, supplanted the need for additional security, and nothing had been done. How about the factoid: The Benghazi Consulate was and is sovereign territory. President Obama has a responsibility and honor duty to defend this situation.

President Obama's once march toward the election has been called "bumps in the road." September 11, 2012, was the infamous date that described he would executed a plan on a diplomatic facility, where the political example of improvised explosive devices (IED) blowing thereby gives the accessibility of the Obama record as "commander-in-chief." This evidence gives us the proof that engaging Islamists are controlling the Middle East. While Diplomat Christopher Stevens was liaison to the opposition in Libya, the President of the United States (POTUS) was arming them, including Jihadist Abdelhakim Belhadj, the leader of the party Libyan Islamic Fighting Group. The weapons were in the dangerous grasping hands of Benghazi. This shipment was part of a zealously miscue because it gives a sleazy construction that enforces the Iran/Contra or say nothing of the Operation Fast & Furious!

Investigative journalists once reported that administration people had nothing to do with the "consulate in Benghazi" and he called it a "shabby" nondescript building that lacked major defense protection.

Stevens' last official act was to cement plans with a diplomat from Turkey. From this source was an additional shipment to al Qaeda and Syria. In other words, a central role was attempted to Jihadists to fight the presidential regime in Syria. Also there were two large warehouses with the consulate where their contents were disclosed. Anyway, the shipment went through Saudi Arabia and Qatar to supply the Syrian rebels. By and large, this so-called President Obama has been entering into conflict and gun walking on a large scale. This explains the country's desperate bid to mislead voting people through his serial deflections of Benghazi Gate.

On September 14, CNN correspondents found Ambassador Stevens' diary at the site of the attack several days before. Stevens expressed his need for help involving al Qaeda presence in the area, plus his being on their list. Later CNN was accused of piracy and breaking promises to the family that would not appear on the diary. After a meeting to discuss the deteriorating security situation at Benghazi, embassy officials sent a cable specifying the needs will be discussed at a later date. After reading it, Army General Ham (head of African command) phoned Stevens and asked if the command needed a special team. Stevens replied no and repeated no at the meeting in Germany with AFRICOM in his command post. Ham offered again but Stevens responded no.

America will soon have to believe that there is a scandal covering all of the bullshit that this Obama Administration has been telling behind closed doors about the Benghazi interaction and its bumbling aftermath. The White House and the State Department orchestrated by Hillary Clinton knew well that the Benghazi encounter was inspired by the al Qaeda right from the get go! Drawing from the start, there is new evidence that they were expecting this attack for months.

According to one individual, we have one decision: Leave Benghazi or you will be killed. Lieutenant Colonel Andy Wood was a top security man who met with Ambassador Stevens every day. In June, three months before the attack, al Qaeda tried to assassinate the British ambassador. Wood said the attack came as no surprise to him. With online postings, al Qaeda was saying that they would attack the Red Cross, the British, and the Americans in Benghazi. As they attacked the Red Cross and the British Mission, they antagonized each other, realizing that it was going to happen. We included our reports to both the State Department and the Department of Defense. Andy Wood the Ambassador Stevens three months before the compound was overrun!

Andy Wood made it clear that you are going to be attacked and you need to change your security profile. Basically your operation should change localities within the city. Be flexible and the terrorists are keeping an eagle eye on you. The final attack can be verifiably dependent on these facilities.

Abu Anas al-Libni was known by the U.S. He was working with others to establish a secret terrorist within this country. Al-Libni was wanted for his role in the bombing of two U.S. Embassies in Africa.

In view of the critically of things belonging to the night in Libya, my thrust is that Secretary Clinton and President Obama had all of the intelligence warning them of an attack in Benghazi. These repartee are not only for the whistleblowers who were talking about such an attack in the city. Gregory Hicks gave singularly damaging testimony to Congress, but the White House continued to turn the other eye and obfuscate any attempts to gain the truth.

We continue to plead representatives of Congress for answers about the murders of American citizens overseas. The complicity of President Obama and Secretary Clinton in the deaths and cover-ups of these four Americans deserve the exact reason of death, rather than forgetting what happened in Libya in 2012.

At 11:10 P.M. and 5:10 P.M. eastern time, the drone begins video feed to Washington, D.C., Secretary Clinton at 5:41 eastern time sent an order to the CIA Deputy Director Bluaeus to coordinate. The CIA was made up of U.S. persons, yet had a ten-member security team at the annex and the State Department could assist the consulate if such an attack was inevitable. On September 12, the president condemned "the outrageous attack" on U.S. diplomatic facilities. The secretary of state stood by him! He faulted the 9/11 attacks and indicated that last night we learned of the heinous attack in Benghazi! President Obama went on to say that we would continue to explore, evaluate, to see justice is done for this depressing state of violence. "And make no mistake, justice will be done." Finally he ordered all security measures would be invoked worldwide. Additionally he sent fifty Marines Fast Attack Team members to bolster the area that is free from further danger there. The FBI would send a team there for investigating the attack. The Benghazi timeline is brought out in a campaigning even as terrorist forces demolished the compound in Libya. The State Department was warned six months ago of the wants and needs of this unprotected compound.

Secretary of State Clinton said on September 12, 2012, that the perpetrators were heavily armed and were a "small and savage force." She invoked at the internet that took place in Cairo, Egypt, as an uprising to either or suggest that this was not a time for violence. They dispatched two Arleigh Burke Class Destroyers (it was not identified who ordered them), which were sent to Libya along with the unmanned drones to search for the attackers. September 12, 2012, in golden Colorado, the president paid tribute to the four Americans killed in the poorly diplomatic port in Benghazi. He stated that no act of violence would go unpunished. In a press briefing on September 14, the White House secretary told reporters that we do not have concrete evidence that heinous act was not in reaction to the film. His speech was so flawed with missing data that this attack was not preplanned. All in all, this is not a reaction to a 9/11 anniversary that we know of!

On September 14, the remains of four victims were flown in to Andrews AFB, Maryland. There the president and Secretary of State Hillary Clinton attended the ceremony. Death surrounded the few as four flag-draped caskets with military honors paraded the few heartbroken viewers. On September 16, U.S. Ambassador Susan Rice appeared on five major interviews where, according to her, she got the "talking points" from a CIA memo! Incapable of providing an "honest assessment," she indicated that extremists participated in violent demonstrations. What a crock of baloney! Incidentally violence is taken from the Bible; it means terrorism on September 18, 2012. The president and the secretary stated that there was no evidence that the assault was preplanned. That is all we know of the mismatch! On September 20, Carney, the Press secretary, let it slip from his lips that it was self-evident that Benghazi was a terrorist attack.

On September 25, 2012, before the United Nations' grand assembly, the USA president stated that these attacks on our civilians and attacks on Americans will no doubt rest when we track down killers and bring them to justice. On the same date in September, the secretary of state said a possible link between al Qaeda and the Maghab ties in with the Benghazi forces.

THE STATE DEPARTMENT

The State Department, required by the Omnibus Diplomatic and Antiterrorism Act of 1986, launched on October 4, 2012, "to examine the facts and circumstances of the attacks." Four members of the board were selected by Clinton and another by the Director of National Intelligence. James R. Clapper and Ambassador Thomas Pickering was the chairman of the aggregate group. On December 20, 2012, a report was released that was a sharp criticism of the State Department for ignoring requests for guards, safety upgrades, and overall security techniques to a falling lack of a safe environment. It went on to say that systems' failures in leadership, management deficiencies at senior levels within the State Department. Benghazi was nowhere guarded nor was this consulate protected from such an onslaught.

The new year started with a cannonball falling over the financial mountain with an outbreak of selfish motive. Now is the time for any good woman, meaning Secretary of State Hillary Clinton, to take the stand. The irony of this is she will do anything to avoid testifying about September 11, 2012. Secretary of states fall and get a concussion, a blood clot via her brain and skull, some TV hosts think that she precluded to duck out of these Congressional hearings on the attack on the U.S. Diplomatic compound in Libya. An independent report revealed placed responsibility on the State Department. The week security of the Benghai compound was lying heavily on additional manpower, yet this protection had been failed or ignored. One writer demanded her hospital records. John Bolton, formally an ambassador to the United Nations, named Clinton's case a "diplomatic illness," which could avoid questions of Benghazi.

Immediately after the fact, Hillary Clinton stood next to the president as the Marines carried these flag-draped caskets from the airplane at Andrews Air Force Base. Annoyed by complaints about the initial attack, she rose to the occasion to protect United States Ambassador Susan Rice. It was she who vilified for widely claims that carried out the raid rather than terrorism. She took all responsibility for the heinous event, which Republicans accused her of the sword trick to protect the president. Eventually she will step forward and the nation clearly needs to know what happened at Benghazi.

At last a Homeland Security and Government Affairs Committee Chairman Joe Lieberman and Ranking Member Susan Collins reported on December 30, 2012, that there was a high rise of terrorist attacks on the United States' employees in the compound in Benghazi. The attack on its mission should have caused the State department to take adequate steps, but the State failed to take immediate action to reduce the mission's downfall!

On January 23, 2013, Secretary of State Clinton clashed with fiery answers to Republican questions of Obama if the Benghazi frecas. At times she was quiet spoken when the Congressional hearings tried to mislead the country when the ambassador and the Navy Seals were killed. She insisted that the State Department would move with great speed to strengthen inept security at Embassies worldwide. She took responsibility for the department's failures, eventually to this assault. The repeated attempts for more security at Benghazi never reached her desk, but her signature was on every message! Her voice cracking at one point, she said the attack and subsequent tragedies of family members were in a grip. Question: Why was Clinton wearing the horrific coke-like horned-rimmed glasses? This perhaps explains her defiance and willingness to chastise members of Congress during five hours or more hours during two separate bodies.

In the Congressional hearings, Senator Ron Johnson pressed Clinton that we were misled concerning protests and assaults grew out of that. This offered a response that we had only four dead Americans, with her voice quivering with hate as both she and Johnson spoke over one another.

She totally bypassed Senator Rand Paul, who stated, "If I had been president, and you did not read the cables from Benghazi and from Ambassador Stevens, I would have relieved you of your post." Clinton repeated that requests for additional security did not come to her level. Four senior State Department officials had been relieved of their duties. Upon asked instantly about this incident, Republican Jeff Duncan challenged Clinton's claim with "clear eyes," saying she would have personally insured security at the mission. Finally he commented that she had let the consulate become a death camp since nothing was done to protect it from terrorist attacks.

HOUSE SELECTS INVESTIGATION COMMITTEE

Republican Trey Gowdy, from South Carolina, questioned a witness during the House oversight in the Government Reform committee, insisting the Obama Administration is covering up deadly information about the Benghazi attack on September 11, 2013. During Wednesday's hearing, he questioned Greg Hicks, former Deputy Chief of Missions at the embassy in Tripoli. The South Carolina Congressman read previously a released email sent by a State Department identifying a terrorist group the day after it occurred. Hicks was shocked as the attack was initially blamed on a video! Gowdy followed with the president of Libya in an attack with terror links. Hicks recalled that he did remember the president of Libya calling a spontaneous protest. When Congressman Gowdy asked if the ambassador talked to you, what did the dying man say to you? Greg responded, "Yes, we are all under attack." When asked about the U.S. Ambassador Rice's talk shows in blaming the attack on an anti-Muslim YouTube video, Mr. Hicks was completely stunned. "My jaw dropped and I was embarrassed," he replied. Hicks also replied that he made no attempts to talk to Rice before speaking on TV on Sunday.

Gowdy later showed an email sent by Beth Jones, the acting security for Middle Eastern affairs at the State Department. Some of these events have not been released.

Speaker Boehner for seventeen months has not set up the establishment of an official committee on the Battle of Benghazi. A second letter, which was sent to Boehner, had ninety-four patriotic Americans requesting he authorize a House Select Investigation Committee. This select group and only this bodacious gathering can issue the subpoenas required. Obama has classified this as preventing the House from getting to the bottom of why Obama refused to issue "Cross Border Authority," preventing launching waiting on the runway 458 miles in Italy and within 90 minutes of flight time or 2 hours from Benghazi.

Former Chairman of the Joint Chiefs of Staff Admiral Mike Mullen was appointed by Hillary Clinton to participate in the Accountability Review Board (ARB). In presenting the facts internally bypassed the fact that Obama refused to release the "Cross Border Authority." In another case, he never interviewed the apparent central figure that was responsible for the U.S. Mission in Benghazi: Hillary Clinton. Clinton, despite personal cables and phonecon at least eight times a day nearly over a six-month period by the Ambassador Stevens, the CIA, the DIA, and Libyan State Security, confirmed that security was dangerously inadequate. Ambassador Stevens was on the al Qaeda hit list with many camps nearly with the U.S. Mission in apparent danger. Clinton refused to authorize a contract with the ambassador to fund his personal Security Detail. Systemic failure was prevalent at the State Department, which during Hillary Clinton's juncture was fraudulent in respect to inadequate security inaccuracy in Benghazi!

The House Committee of Investigation met in chambers with Trey Gowdy (R-SC), grilling Admiral Mullen, Retired, for the correct answers.

1. First, Trey asked him, did he interview her by submitting written questions for her response? Admiral's answer was no.

2. Did the secretary know of the attacking the Middle East meaning Benghazi? The answer was yes and no.

3. Trey's next question was security, was this discussed? The problem was twofold, whereby Admiral Mullen was not sure even when the Ambassador complained over the last six months.

4. In 1998, Mr. Gowdy brought up the Accountability Review Board (ARB), which recommended that each secretary of state personally review these sites. Did the secretary of state review these documents? The admiral's reply was he was not sure.

5. The speaker asked if he considered closing these or even Benghazi. The result was the admiral did not interview her.

Trey Gowdy asks two questions. Who said this? The ARB was well documented and the admiral said no, the secretary of state said that! Gowdy asked another question that was quoted. The president said that, which the admiral failed both questions!

Consolidate for the Secretary of State Sherald Miller has been a lawyer for Hillary Clinton. For some unknown reason, she has been given a "heads up." He asked the admiral, did she tell the truth during her tenure? Therefore, she was a fact witness! The admiral was slow to react, but Trey and the admiral agreed that there are good and bad fact lawyers!

Michael Morell, a former CIA Deputy Director, was called into the Senate House Intelligence session. The controversy over which was he truthfully gave the (woman who is in the president snell) gave the Saturday/Sunday testimony that the Benghazi attack was not a terror attack but fictitious. Mr. Morell was fairly pushed to take advantage of this, yet the videotape side, he did not!

We now have evidence that the State Department knew that Benghazi was a jihad terrorist attack. We know that Susan Rice, Hillary Clinton, and Barack Obama knew and lied to the American people. The Democrats are attempting to boycott a select committee based on emails that an infamous smoking gun released by Ben Rhodes. This is a slow bulk proof that the White House is the leader of this twenty-one-month cover-up. This presidential assault on one Constitution and freedom was Obama's fall into the depths of muck, which is his primary response to the Islamist attack on September 11, 2012. This is not the end of this controversy, as Susan Rice gave as a talking point emanating or were driven by 1500 Pennsylvania Avenue!

In reviewing the forty some new documents, there are sections that are blacked out. One may wonder why all this white-out caused the paragraphs to be redacted. Many still or when this happened, a memo from Payton Knopf clearly gives the clock a timeline, which the State Department Victoria calls "it was clearly a complex attack."

The president started his weekly meeting with the secretary of defense and the chairman of the joint chiefs. This ironically had scaled back daily intelligence briefs, whereby the president only met occasionally about half the time. According to the subject matter, each distinguished member was told it was a terrorist attack. So why did Obama dream up a false narrative and why did the defense participants speak out?

Then we come to the death of Ambassador Stevens, and the president was not notified until the next morning. If the president was asleep, he would be awakened and told of his tragic death. Why are they covering up when Obama was informed of the ambassador's death?

In the same email, Knopf asked the State Department who perpetrated the attack. Ansar al-Sharia was taking credit for the hellacious attack. Therefore, every person knew that the al Qaeda-linked group was behind the compound attack in Benghazi. State Department Dan Fogarty advised all the February 17 Brigade was responding to the mission attack. This group is a jihadist militia. Thus as always, this militia, which has the best armed and technologically advanced, might outsource their response to a jihadist organization.

Questions: Did the FBI release Christopher Stevens' autopsy? How precisely did he die? And where was the President of the United States on the night of September 11, 2012?

House Speaker John Boehner appointed seven Republicans and five Democrats to the board tasked with continuing investigations of the 2012 attack in Benghazi. The chairman of this agust group is Representative Trey Gowdy of South Carolina. The other Republicans are Susan W. Brooks of Indiana, Jim Jordan of Ohio, Mike Pompeo of Kansas, Martha Roby of Alabama, Peter Roskam of Illinois, and Lynn Westmoreland of Georgia. The Democrat five will be Elijah Cumming of Maryland, Adam Smith of Washington State, Adam Schiff from California, Linda Sanchez from California, and Tammy Duckworth from Illinois. This group will question subpoenas and will offer a united front on the unanswered questions of the attack on Benghazi.

Last summer (2013), the president gave a speech that blamed on phony scandals. In his speech he pleaded to reverse the trend in distractions. This is Washington's highest priority to quell political posturing and phony digs that take away what we need to do to show up the middle class.

Where dunderhead Jay Carney was asked, "Can you tell us what phony scandals he's talking about?" Jay frolicked about mimicking words about partisan scandals, whether attacks in Benghazi are the answer, and about the IRS scuttlebutt, attempts to turn these subjects into full-blown issues have failed.

Benghazi is not a phony or lies in the deep smoldering for twenty months! This administration has lied through its teeth. The truth must be known of four Americans who were killed from the beginning to the end of their deaths.

1. The story of the Benghazi slaying was a lie from the moment it was told. Secretary of State Hillary Clinton was the perpetrator!

2. The day after the attack, Ben Rhoads, the apparatchik, charged with the coordination and administration's talking points on September 11, 2012. He stated that the attack was not related to the internet video "Innocence of Muslims." This was an executed/coordinated attack. This opinion was verified by a USAF Brigadier General Robert Lovell, who was in USAFRICOM during the attack, and by CIS Director Michael Morrell in the Congressional testimony.

3. Despite this for pay, the administration put out a blatant lie to the Congress and the American people. The reason was they were only sixty days from a presidential election; they could not answer any questions. The lying continues this very day. Jay Carney, David Plouffe, and perhaps Dave Weigel, by insisting that the deaths of four Americans has already been explained, is "impenetrable."

FINAL ANALYSIS

1. The commander-in-chief knew Benghazi would be attacked: Americans will have to realize that scud hiding in September 11, 2012, is the peddling of bull excrement covering up the Benghazi turmoil and the deadly aftermath. The White House and the State Department (headed by Hillary Clinton) knew the Benghazi attack headed by al Qaeda right from the start. New evidence shows that they were expecting the attack for months.

2. Andy Wood had one option: "Leave Benghazi or you will be killed." Green Beret Commander Lieutenant Colonel Andy Wood was based in Tripoli, where he met daily with Ambassador Stevens. He was in Benghazi in June 2012, when al Qaeda tried to assassinate the British ambassador. Using a similar tactic, al Qaeda used the Red Cross and then the Americans in Benghazi. They knew Washington was aware because it was monitored and included our reports went to the State Department and the

Department of Defense. Wood's device was to the point; he told Stevens that in three months the United States Consignment would be overrun. Woods insisted that you need to change your security profile, move out temporarily, change location, and they are watching your every move in final planning stages before September 11, 2012. We must demand the truth from our representatives!

3. All of the evidence the president and the secretary of state in the cover-ups and the deaths of these four brave Americans is locked in an intelligence safe. With proper taking care of the shabby consulate without proper security, they would still be alive.

4. The long-delayed Senate Intelligence Committee report revealed that it faulted the State Department and associated intel for not preventing attacks on two facilities in Benghazi, which brought about the killing of four Americans.

5. The bipartisan report laid out a dozen findings of assaults on a compound and Central Intelligence Agency (CIA) in the city. The State Department plus the CIA failed to increase security despite six months of warnings and blamed intelligence, who did not share data about the existence of the CIA outpost within the U.S. military. Among other factors, United States Military Command in Africa did not know of the CIA Annex, and the Pentagon did not have the capability to defend the State Department compound in an emergency crisis! These attacks were preventable and based on terrorist activity in Libya. Thus the shortfalls of security at the mission were not excluded based on extensive reporting. The report said that the CIA and State were not working together. The statement meant the CIA and well-trained contractors and elite United States forces were not in location of the mission in the event of a crisis.

6. Attackers used "diesel fuel" to set the main building aflame. According to testimony, a member of the National Counter-Terrorism led U.S. Ambassador Stevens to an open escape window at the compound. Nearing being unconscious, he opened the escape hatch and crawled out. He searched the building multiple times. The DS agent climbed a ladder and when he reached the roof, he contacted other DS agents. The committee found that the military response was safe and hindered.

7. The State Department issued an update to improve all facets of security and make other improvements recommended by an oversight panel. State Department spokeswoman Marie Harf cited that the reports had little information and that does not do much to expand the government's analysis of the attacks.

8. This document contains only one mention of Secretary of State Hillary Rodman Clinton, who is ultimately responsible for the failures of Benghazi. The committee said there was no specific warning when lack of data about this happening was because of lack of the outpost defense.

9. The result of the recent public and finger pointing at the Barack Obama and Hillary Clinton, they knew that the attack of September 11, 2012, was of a terrorist nature. Why in heaven's name did they not do anything about it? No help was sent. Why did they make a statement that one knows is false, and should both continue to perverse the truth and to blame themselves for this tragic happening?

10. President Obama was in the political fight, as he was campaigning throughout the United States of America. He wanted Hillary Clinton to say something—anything—at the time of the attack to appease those four dead men on the ground. Yet she still gets credit for her bid for the White House in 2016.

11. Not a pretty sight, Secretary of State Hillary Clinton! This man should come home at Christmas time but because of you, never again. I hope his family members will follow you deep down inside of you as you look at a person in uniform or stand under an American flag. May God judge you for your sins against you and your fellow countrymen.

CHAPTER 6

THE INTERNAL REVENUE SERVICE

The United States Internal Revenue Service (IRS) in 2013 said that it had targeted political or otherwise groups applying for tax-exemption status. The revealing status was closer security based or their logos were used for political means. U.S. Attorney General Eric Holder led this probe as part of a criminal way of this gender. Apparently this led to public and political targeting to conservative groups known as "tea parties." Further scrutiny showed plenty that certain terms, objectives, or themes brought in "occupy movements," which set in motion a use that establishes as a goal that compiles a list through May 2013.

The U.S. Federal Tax law exempts certain nonprofit organizations, thus they do not have to pay this tax. The tax code permits each organization only if they are exclusively for the promotion of social welfare. The verifiable definition had made the U.S. tax / treasury confusing, and as a result the IRS permits many loopholes, which some organizations engage in lobbying or campaigning activities that are not left in the deep primary activity. Chris Hollen suggested a lawsuit against the IRS, which stops the tradition of allowing groups registered under "501 C." Therefore, the IRS was against protect organizations as nonprofit groups dedicated to social welfare keep from having to post the names of donors or the amount of dollars the individuals have totally.

On January 21, 2010, the U.S. Supreme Court decided that this overturned previous restrictions on political spending and allowed unlimited spending, which often spends a great amount of money giving other groups to weigh future elections. Some Tea Party members began forming committees as offshoots vis-à-vis 501 © tax exempt organized groups. In September 2010, these groups have spent almost one hundred million dollars more than double the money spent in the election four years earlier. *The New York Times* reported that the biggest players have been the 501 C components and these purchasers have been heavily Republicans. Really, the pouring of money led into political runoffs!

Shortly therefore, Senate House Democrats continued the IRS to investigate the abuses of Tax Exempt Status engaged in political mumbo-jumbo in early 2012. A letter was sent regarding this mishap. A second missile was sent proclaiming that the IRS clearly states the amount of political activity for social welfare groups to require these groups to document their percentage of their company that is dedicated to social welfare. It is necessary that these groups are to notify these doors what percentage of donations must be claimed for tax deductions. Senators promised to accomplish these goals if the IRS did not do these criteria by issuing new administrative rules.

Facing a possible dismissal, the IRS coming close to a party scandal, retired Monday leaving one chapter untold in a ruckus that has burned the tax-collection agency since spring. Lois Lerner headed the IRS section, which handled first the tax-exempt status when she was placed on leave in May 2013. From 2010 and 2012 she improperly had agents targeting tea party groups when they applied for tax-exempt status.

This staff, group, or whatever you call it was also in charge of medical records and stuff. The IRS will be there helping you make decisions of your own medical problems—tyranny, is it a thing of the past? Really! Tyranny is using the IRS as a weapon. In other words, the IRS flags 2012 political groups to see if they were violating tax-exempt criteria. Lois Learner signals out the characters' "tea party" and patriots in the applications. In some cases they were asked the donors which is a no-no in the IRS Bible! She acknowledges that was incorrect about that's not the way we select cases for review according to Lois Lerner.

Remember when we used to mock those who warned against U.S. tyranny? Well, take a backseat as the Obama quike used the IRS to ban communications and harass them. Everyone was getting a letter from the IRS. Lois Lerner was responsible for this, as she was in charge of the group that forces the tax-exempt agencies, which included the word "tea party" or "patriot" was singled out for other reviews.

Lerner first disclosed the targeting in May and was asked a planted question about the IRS treatment of political groups. She refused to answer any questions at a congressional hearing. Her constitutional right was not to incriminate herself. Immediately she was placed on leave.

The board found "neglect of duties" during her tenure as director of exempt organization. She also mismanagement with or upon review by the Inspector General's report. The Republicans called for a fine, but the IRS confirmed her retirement stating she has no longer preventing her from commenting an individual employee.

The more evidence contained in the emails gives credibility of Lois Lerner and other IRS officials blame the targeting is directed from Washington, D.C. Furthermore the directing is not coming from Cincinnati employees as Obama says it is so fond of the truth.

The Washington Examiner details in July 2012 that Holly Pax asked IRS lawyer Steven Grodnitzky to inform Cindy (director of EO in Cincinnati) and Sharon (manager in Los Angeles) knew that we have been handling tea party applications for numerous months. Grodnitzky, who worked the IRS Exempt Organization Technical Unit, responded to Paz that they had been a tea party in conjunction with Cincy. The applications are being developed in Washington and are providing copies with the background to be used in their cases. In February 2010, Thomas directed to let Washington be informed of political implications regarding the tea party organization. This is a high-profile case.

Lois Lerner attempted to soften the blow of the scandal. BOLO implies specific elects with the tea party movement. John Shafer wonders what fault will be used to label tea party cases. Does a statement specify tea party? The screening group asks how the employees are supplying BOLO shorthand mention of the party. The following are criteria within BOLO tea party references:

1. "Tea Party," Patriots, or 9/12 Project.
2. Government spending or debt and taxes.
3. Educate the public and make America a great place to live.
4. Critical in the case file as how the country is being run.

Lois Lerner wrote on April 2, 2013, that we believe we have provided info that shows that no one in the EO "developed" the criteria. Rather, staff used their own interpretations of the brief reference to "organizations involved with the Tea Party movement," which was on the BOLO list. If that doesn't show evidence of a conspiracy, I give up!

Ousted IRS acting chief Steve Miller and former IRS Commissioner Douglas Shulman testified during a Senate Finance Committee hearing on May 22, 2013. The former top official of the Internal Revenue Service said that he was dismayed that an inspector's general report during his tenure, the agency blew scrutinized conservative groups seeking tax-exempt position.

Douglas Shulman, who was the organization for five years before retiring in November 2013, along with Steve Miller, who succeeded him as acting IRS leader, and J. Russell George, the treasury inspector general appeared with the Senate Finance Committee on Tuesday, May 21, 2013. As a note, Miller and

George testified before the House Ways and Means committee last week. Committee chairman Boucers D – Montana asked Miller and Shulman why firmer action wasn't taken to address political targeting. Both gentlemen denied knowledge of such. Shulman could not answer a culture of indifference arouse at the IRS.

Both members under investigation sore that these ridiculous failure was the fault of the lower-level managers who failed to establish the severity of the problem.

Senator Orrin Hatch pressed both men about why they did not inform Congress about the problem that were coming from the Cincinnati office. Shulman indicated that he made known in the Spring of 2012 that such items as "tea party" were used to identify key groups for additional examination. Until an audit came out, he did not have a full trump until he was able to assimilate the few set of facts!

Also summoned in this congressional case were plans to invoke his rights against self-incrimination and declined to testify at this hearing. Lois Lerner heads the IRS division but has singled conservative groups for extra scrutiny. She was to commanded to testify and to appear in the Congress oversight group, yet she refused to offer any data because of a possibility that is because a criminal investigation by the Justice Department. Meanwhile, the tea party activists wave flags, sing, and chant outside federal buildings in several United States tea party sites. The mystery man opened the doors the mornings by a story from Washington, D.C. The House Ways and Means Committee unfounded an unidentified IRS agent, which said the agency is still targeting conservatives. These were the months where it was known three months ago! His remarks came from a closed-door hearing, which was made public in response to questioning. The agent responded that tea groups were seeking tax-exempt credibility but were subject to "secondary screening" in his office.

The IRS is up to no good! They are still out to get the tea party, but why? Congress isn't even united against the tea party. The GOP wants to torpedo the party, as if one is brushing another under the rug. Over and over the tea party will continue to be targeted!

How about the IRS scandal? This is about transforming political dissent and how the government deals with political corruption. Scandal specifically shows the nudge from intimidation encouragement to trust known sources with a sense of security, like al Jazeera and the *Huffington Post*, is to shoot where the IRS will use a weapon to get the finances and fame.

We have gone from nudge to shove, which destroys you and the union thugs to beat you. Next the IRS will bankrupt you and when it comes to the kind of gun the IRS has it will go after the American people. At most, the AP scandal is transforming the media.

It is a fact that the president has and is prosecuting more whistleblowers than all combined in American history. He has clearly prosecuted more covert speakers than all combined presidents. World War I, World War II, Vietnam, and Lincoln and the Civil War. To transform the media, you have to guard the property and when these fail, you intimate or assail the press until they are unwilling to cooperate.

This challenge is the last part of the fundamental transformation. What does it have in common? Transformation. Transform the Middle East, the First Amendment, and the medium and the watchman. Transform means let's an act that would contain the United States of America.

Mass corruption in the IRS means that people who disagree with the government are analyzed by them, but you are definitely wrong! The president says, "not a smidgen of corruption."

During the Super Bowl briefing of the president, Bill O'Reilly of Fox News, Obama blamed the wrongdoing on the IRS. Fox News has been negligent in reporting publicizing of the scandal. He touts the investigation has cleared the IRS, but in reality, isn't one federal agency to investigate another bureaucrat like have a fox digging his way to the henhouse?

According to our new Fearless Leader, our own silly American people don't understand. In other words, there have been multiple hearings on it, and when you have got 501 (c)24 law people think it is confusing.

Recently, the Obama clientele quietly ordered the IRS to cut down the outbreak of its opponents by imposing new regulations on nonprofit groups and its Christian groups. There rules forbid conservative distributing vote guides, scorecards, and legislative or even tallying voters. Naturally all Big Labor unions are free of this requirement. We must stop this attack on freedom of speech and defeat regulations to end Christian and Tea Party Americans! If we sign up now, we can defeat our petition to Congress and the Obama machine.

This pro-family non-profiles must be muzzled against the Christians and Conservatives to be informed and should vote. Even worse, Obama has exempted deep-pocketed literal units like SEIU or AFL-CIO from these crippling regulations.

With more than 700,000 members and supporters, we have the largest collection of conservative voters. We had one mission at hand: Stop Obama and his radical non-Christian agenda for America. In 2014 will be no different as we plan to distribute 33 million voter rights and will make over 21 million phone calls to cement Christian voter turnout. We, the voters, must turn back the IRS's radical ban on Christians and conservations free speech.

This week, May 11, 2014, the House of Representatives voted and placed Lois Lerner in contempt. A year after learning that she is a bureaucrat that was in charge is finally being held responsible. Lois Lerner was head of the IRS's tax-exempt office and oversaw the targeting politically run organizations. In America the government should not spare their people based on their views.

Lois Lerner would not let her views come clean to the United States citizens. That's why the representatives listened to 20,000 messages and are determined to get answers. Some Progressives tried to ignore the IRS scandal goal. Some wanted this degradation of law to change the TV channel, while others broke through the media and made a difference. The IRS should not be allowed to get by with harassing our citizens based on political beliefs. Thus holding Lois Lerner in contempt of Congress is a vital step in making targets of Conservatives again.

That being said, the good folks at IRS aren't out to get us if we are not a conservative group like Christians, the Tea Party, and anti-abortion followers or anyone who offends the current organization.

CHAPTER 7

NATIONAL SECURITY AGENCY

The National Security Agency (NSA) is the main producer and manager of signals intelligence for the United States of America. NSA operates in terms of personnel and budget is the largest community and operates under the jurisdiction of the Defense and reports to the Direction of National Intelligence. NSA is authorized to accomplish its mission through clandestine means by cutting in electronics systems. It also is engaging in sabotage utilizing subversive software! And one other thing, NSA is active in protection of all communications and information data.

Unlike the Defense Intelligence Agency (DIA) and the Central Intelligence Agency (CIA), both which specialize in foreign human espionage. Although the USA is not collected human-source intelligence, it provided with the coordination/reconfiguration of SIGNET components. Non-SIGNET government organizations are prevented for engaging in these activities without the approval of the NSA by way of the Defense Secretary.

History reveals that NSA was the Armed Forces Security Agency (AFSA) created on May 20, 1949. AFSA was to direct Defense communications and electronic intelligence sites, except those of U.S. military units. AFSA failed to do this task plus other coordinated with civilian compounds that shared their interests. On December 10, 1951, the president signed or ordered a panel of distinguished personnel to correct AFSA's failures. The Brownell Report established the strength and resulted it being called the National Security Agency.

Beginning in June 2013, disclosures were made to the media revealing massive spying, both foreign and domestic. Most of these leaks were to Edward Snowden. It was revealed that:

- Over a billion people worldwide are intercepted by phone or internal communications.

- Extensive espionage was against governments in Europe, South America, and Asia, plus the European Union as well as the United Nations!

- 120 million Verizon subscribers are examined, as well as Google, Microsoft, Facebook, and many other meta-data. Their act according to The Patriot Act whereby all recordings may be considered relevant to terrorism. Only a small minority of this data-set may relate to terror.

- Successful weakening of excessive software and internet companies, has made NSA more vulnerable to the attackers.

- NSA intercepts are received by DEA and IRS, plus other enforcement agencies. Federal agents are then told to cover up or "recreate" the investigative trail to hide where it had originated.

- Most members of Congress were unaware how these systems originated. Therefore, most of Congress were not permitted to view, thus have a basic need to know. Clearly, the FISC court claimed the NSA activities does not have the capability to know about them.
  Numerous uprising stories have removed their ugly heads as Obama's

Administration was broadcast in the media:

On March 20, 2013, Director of Naval Intelligence Admiral James Clapper stated before Congress that NSA does not collect data on millions or hundreds of millions of Americans. On June 9 he retracted his former statement and said only meta-data of phone or intercept data are collected, but neither are actual message contents.

On July 31, 2013, NSA Director acknowledges Clapper's statement that no emails or phone contact was generated. Almost the same day, the NSA X Keyscope program does collect millions of emails of U.S. citizens without authorization. General Keith Alexander stated that it recorded anything that a user does on the internet. The general admitted that the stored data was never analyzed; however, the message will be dissected when reference to al Qaeda or if it involved in any other terrorist groups.

On June 27 the director of NSA stated that the bulk of phone/internet intercepts preventing 54 terrorist events, including 13 in the USA. These tapes provided the "unravel the threat stream." NSA John Anglis conferred to the Senate that there intercepts did not seem vital to shutting down terrorist attacks. But the four San Diego men were close to ending and convicting Al-Shabocab, a militia conducting terrorism in Somalia.

On August 9, 2013, President Obama responded that alleged content is collected, legal checks which preclude access of information means no examples of abuse. Drip by drip, once a week utilization requires maximum attention and they can catch one at some second, not at all precise.

On October 1 many companies and trade groups signed a letter supports bills that more details about government's secret requests. These bills will solidify more options where and how often they received national security-related requests and provided data to the government

Since then the *Washington Post* reported the NSA began to violate rules that limit access to data thousands of times a year. These spirits of intelligence lead to large-scale interceptions. This building is the tallest building in the National Security Agency complex. The visitor center includes a painting of the NSA seal. Tons of security badges decorate each client and one described it as "a dark glass Rubik's Cube." Snowden has temporary asylum in Russia and has said in terms of personal accomplishment he has achieved a victory. Journalists have worked hard but still everything has he validated. His techniques have caused an exposure of NSA's data-mining in the United States as well as the international community. Snowden has access to the "Black Budget," where the U.S. spends money on its intelligence efforts. Some call him a traitor, a whistleblower, and a patriot. The debate continues, yet his revelations of mass surveillance could bring about the end of this program.

On January 6, 2011, a groundbreaking ceremony will be held to begin construction on NSA's first Comprehensive National Cyber-Security Initiative (CNCI) Data Center or "Utah Data Center." It is being built at Camp Williams, which is twenty-five miles south of Salt Lake City. It is expected to be complete or operational by September 2013.

The U.S. Army Corps of Engineers and National Security Agency offered a groundbreaking ceremony for the first comprehensive National Cyber-security Initiative Data Center on January 6, 2011, at Camp Williams. This 1.5 billion-dollar NSA data center is an important establishment in Utah's public esteem as a major technology center. This building will provide approximately 8,000 jobs during construction. Once completed the estimate of 200 high-paid employees will round out this facility.

Officially named the Utah Data Center, the volumes of data have earned the nickname "Spy Center," the first in the U.S.A. Information collecting program. A White House document points a serious economic and NSA issues, but as a government we are not prepared to counter. Technology-related countermeasures often bend or denial the real purpose of cyber related issues.

President Obama has identified cyber-security as one of the national security challenges we face as a nation. As president he ordered a thorough review of all programs, secret or above, and set forth a program that secures America's digital infrastructure. In May 2009 he received the recommendations of the panel. He then developed a plan where all activities will be conducted whereby privacy rights and civil liberties will be guaranteed in the Constitution and realized by all Americans.

The CNCI promotes the mutually reinforcing goals designed to secure the United States in cyberspace:

- To establish a front line of defense against today's immediate threats, among others, the ability to act and reduce after current vulnerability and present intensions.

- To defend against the full spectrum of threats.

- To strengthen the future of cyber-security environment by developing strategies to deter hostile or malicious activity in cyberspace.

In building this massive structure this could not be constructed without long-term strategic goals within the government. The CNCI was keyed with privacy and civil liberties. These rights of human individuals must remain objectives in this CNCI program. Thus, President Obama declared that transparency is a touchstone of his presidency. Furthermore, he has directed the release of all descriptions of the CNCI!

As technology grows, the NSA's capability to intercept a variety or volume of data will continue to expand. Satellites scoop our calls and emails from the air and beam information to earth receiving stations. One estimate states that each of these bases gather one billion emails, phones calls, and other forms of correspondence every twenty-four hours. The massive surveillance still dominates and will continue in the Obama tender, both home and abroad. The culture of interest reveals intensive hidden environment, which secrecy prevails. For over a decade, Senators Ron Wyden and Mark Udall have been demanding to know how many people have spied on in the U.S. by the NSA. As of yet, no answer has been forthcoming!

A program to permit the NSA to monitor or collect phone records failed in the House. This was a victory for the Obama Administration, which has spent many months defending this vital program. Lawmakers voted to defeat this measure from an unlikely collation of liberal and conservative delegates. As a result, Edward Snowden, a former of NSA contractor, had collected millions of phone records that exceeds the number of records authorized by Congress. The collection, known as Metabase, records where there was a known correction relevant to present investigation. Secret testimony from Foreign Intelligence Surveillance would make available to lawmakers and the court must make available published documents of each opinion for public review.

President Obama will give up his business of swiping up and storing multitudes of data with respect to people's phone calls. The Obama Administration will propose the Congress will take the once secret surveillance that had set off alarms over private concerns and drew sharp criticism in at home and overseas.

The NSA will hold phone companies by keeping records of 18 months. However, this will not work, as NSA will collect data and hold it for 5 years. Change won't happen immediately, but the bulk phone-records program can shut this data after 3 months.

There was little indication that similar measures would have little uprising in the Senate. Obama made it perfectly clear he would veto this proposal. Awash and Conyers agreed to bring the measure to the House floor. Their ability to get 200 votes in the floor was due to the concerns over the NSA's bulk pile of data.

Samsung Smartphones and Dell computers are being tracked by NSA via electronic spy gear. The Christmas warning predicts that Snowden has leaked the document that revifys that claim.

One of the documents Snowden released is a product catalog called the ANT (Access Network Technology) and it has borrowed its way into all architecture made by all major players in the industry. Cisco and its Chinese computer Huowei, producer of mass mailed goods, is equal to U.S. computer Dell.

ANT specializes in Tailored Access Operations commuter remotely asses, monitored by more plexlate data worldwide, which can be murdered by internet that is bugged. NSA can "backdoor" projects in electronics. ANT operations can choose spy gear from a 50-page catalog. Some of the items are:

1. Rigged monitor cable – 30 personal can see what is displayed on the monitor.

2. GMS base station - $40,000 Mimics mobile phone tower and permits single cell phone collection.

3. Computer bugging devices - $1 million

4. Disguised as a normal USB plugs, but really it is capable of sending and receiving data via radio undetected.

Nobody knows that NSA has hacked the system.

U.S. officials have defended the collection and have emphasized that reviews are not listening to American conversations. In fact, the data involved the members detailed and the length of the calls. Before the vote, James Clapper banked the proposal. His endorsement came as Genard Keith Alexandria (NSA head of U.S. Cyber Command) spent hours on Capitol Hill promoting its bill. As an inside, Speaker John Boehner voted against the measure.

Privacy concerns are increasing with people acknowledging their own secret desires are becoming incisive Three quarters of Americans say that half are encroaching on their freedom. The evidence of Americans today believe that the investigation of terrorists threats have doubled in a decade. Today about four in ten say it is paramount to protect privacy that to limit the government's ability to analyze and promote possible terrorist threats.

Only forty-two percent make the United States more safe, yet forty-seven percent see this, quote sabotage, make little difference. With five percent say it makes the nation less safe.

The attacks on the Trade Center on September 11, 2001, were preventable if there had been communication between the intelligence sources. The Patriot Act made it easier to coordinate potential data relating terrorist action. In 2011 President Obama created a four-year extension of three major functions, which allowed wiretaps, business records, and conducting surveillance of "lone wolves," suspected terrorist activities not links to groups.

This surprise is how much we are spending on the name of terrorist. Janet Napolitano, head of the Department of Homeland Security, made statements that certain American groups are as dangerous as radical Islamists. A report circulated by DHS defines "rightwing extremists in the United States" includes racists or hate mongers but also those opposed to abortion and immigration.

Hollywood in films and television shows how government soirees make their living. *The Bourne Identity* and *Enemy of the State* illustrate this. The government is in bed, in that they have indoctrinated everything, bank statements, emails, computer files, phone calls, and every wire and airwave!

CBS has a show, "Person of Interest." The plot of the show is how our data is accessible to the eye! The incredible case is accessing our data, which is easy but Big Brother is watching us.

The internet is a favorite companion! Jobbing with it is a dangerous tool for doing harm. Children must be aware of the targets of evil. One point to make: Pornography has been a sexual desire for sexual assaults.

PRISM is a government spy program that seeks terrorists but it can't seek out criminal activity! Why does government want telephone data? Criminals and others of terrorist use via untraceable pre-paid telephones. There are very few people in either party and now in the administration that are concerned with our National Security.

One could agree that the ruling by a federal judge that the spy program is legal. The headlines on December 27, 2013, came across loud and clear. The federal judge ruled the NSA is legal. This was shocking and sudden to many people because less than two weeks ago the U.S. Circuit Court ruled the exact opposite. The main problem was the collection of phone and email records is unlawful.

In a nutshell, Judge Pauley's rule is very simple whereby the government needs legal right to conduct their insidious programs. Unlike Pauley, he senses that the whole problem of security starts with September 11, 2011!

CHAPTER 8

CUTS JEOPARDIZE NATIONAL SECURITY
ECONOMY – SEQUESTRATION

What caused the nation to prevent falling over the proverbial fiscal cliff? Kicking the physical can down the road! Sequestration begins March 1, 2003, which causes 1.2 trillion in across the board happening.

Now they're saying the president will bow down to the Republicans, but it's their fault. Fifteen percent of the government has been stoked or a unfounded chaos? Let us see what has been sequestered or not. These are a few things we (the people) will have to live through:

- Treatments with children suffering from cancer.
- World War II Memorial – This facility is open 24 hours a day, seven days a week. They put a chain-link fence around the memorial to keep people out.
- Military Chaplains are furloughed; they do not work for free.
- In the Florida Keys small businesses, hunters, and commercial fishermen can no longer practice their trade.
- The American Forces Network 50% of shows half to be liberal.
- The D-day Memorial is closed.
- Mount Vernon – privately funded.
- The president has forced residents out of their homes in Acadia Park, Maine.
- The president has closed the Military Commissary. Military members are shocked when they discover the store's doors are locked.

So the sequential has struck America! The American people are angry by closing privately funds businesses but he can enjoy his favorite golf courses!

The White House members conceived this sequestration plan, which as a drastic series of cuts that were so deep that the Joint Select Committee would be forced to pound out a workable 10-year program reduction. This program was outlined 10 years ago during the 2011 debt ceiling crisis. Political cowardice of the Federal Government, here we are! In some areas the cuts will begin in certain areas and the cuts will begin in nine days. Bloating entitlement programs are gobbling up 56% of our military combination budgets.

Congressional Republicans are willing to let the nation plunge over the embankment. A sequestration has suddenly morphed that the measure will increase the party's position in the budget problems. Paul Ryan steps up and says he blames the impediment train wreck lies wholly on the feet of the Democrats. There appears a little effort to stop this nation from going over the cliff.

Looking back, the Secretary of Defense, Leon Panetta has warned that 500 million dollars will be sliced from the Defense budget over the next 10 years. This is not the only thing it affects: military and national security. Chuck Hagel, Panetta's relief, also has spelled out his concerns. Hagel has addressed to the Senate Armed Services Committee that sequestration will harm readiness and affect each investment program. He also offers to eliminate the sequestration program and pass a deficit reduction plan.

Congress has been unable to pass the 2013 Defense Bill, which includes devastating to military readiness. The Congress has muffled their defensive or offensive hands by offering a yearly plan according to Secretary Hagel.

From the Navy's viewpoint the disaster is a 4.6 billion-dollar loss in operating/maintenance funds. The sea force can add other billions of dollars and possibly it may lose six hundred million dollars equal to major maintenance work scheduled for 30 warships and 250 aircraft. If by March 1, 2003, Congress which is sits idly by, all training flights and exercises will come to a blatant halt. All deploys to the Caribbean and South America will go up in smoke! European deployments will be cut back and the ballistic submarine force will be cut accordingly. Over all the ships and the aircraft will be stopped and the civilian personal might face 22 days of furlough!

The steps that the Military are taking might be reversible. These cuts may well be the harm of evil they will not get. What underway times the combat ships will have. What if an international crisis occurs? Will a carrier group respond in time?

In January Americans have learned the economy and unemployment has inched up and these are signs of sequestration. Eliminating cuts in Defense could be astronomical. Virginia, second only to California in defense spending; however, the state could estimate 207,000 lost jobs.

The major foreign policy issue of the 2000 presidential campaign has been military readiness. A military in decline or in the strongest and the best has been the involuntary of the two parties, the United States readiness has been rejected by comparing with other strategic forces. The measure of how much or how little our forces must be prepared to defeat groups of adversaries in a given war. The evidence is struck forward, our U.S. forces are not ready to handle the nation's national security requirements. The National Security component concludes has the ability to defeat large scale and cross-border aggression. In two theaters is overlapping timeframes. Some generals worry about their forces, which carry out a two-threat war strategy. To prevent war or interaction, a high state of military readiness will deter hostile nations from acting aggressively and therefore preserving peace.

Readiness defined is the ability of a Military Army Division to complete its mission. Next coming the highest achievement versus the lowest level. The highest, operational readiness verifies the low level, which requires manpower, training/equipment, and logistics to meet the challenge. The lower level varies within the military readiness. It could be the deployed country it was recently in, recently leaked documents that nine of twelve military schools were in the lowest readiness grade. The reduction enforces of the U.S. Armed Forces indicate that during 1990 through the Persian Gulf in 1991, the military had been deployed fifty sites. The stream of active duty personnel was reduced 30% and manpower was reduced 16 %; readiness in decline.

> FACT# 1: The size of the U.S. Military has been cut drastically in the past decade.

> Between 1992 and 2000, the Clinton Administration cut more than a half million soldiers and fifty billion in inflated adjusted dollars.

> Reduction in force of the U.S. Military 1992-2000
> 1992, 2000 Percent Change
> Total Active Personnel: 1,913,750 1,371,500 -28%

> Army
>   Active Divisions: 14 10 -29%
>   Reserve Divisions: 10 8 -20%
>   Total Active Personnel: 674,800 469,300 -30%

Navy
    Carrier battle groups: 12 12 0%
    Total ships*: 393 316 -20%
    Total Active Personnel: 546.650 369,800 -32%

Marines
    Expeditionary forces: 3 3 0%
    Total personnel 193,000 171,000 -11%

Air Force
    Active fighter squadrons: 57 52 -9%
    Bomber forces: 270 178 -34%
    Total Active Personnel: 499,300 361,400 -28%

Note: Submarines, surface combatants, patrol and coastal, and amphibious ships.

Source: The international institute for Strategis Studies, *The Military Balance*, 1992 – 1993, pp. 18 – 26, and *The Military Balance*, 1999 -2000, pp. 20 – 26. Also U.S. Department of Defense, The National Defense Budget Estimate for 2001, March 2000, page 207.

In other words, this is what happens to the military force:
Army: lost 4 divisions; two reserve divisions
Air Force: reduced to 52 fighter and 178 bomber forces
Navy: personnel lost 30%; 393 ships to 316 decrease of 20%
Marine: 3 divisions 22,000 active duty lost 11%; Clinton cut 39,000

The effect on readiness is apparent as missions and operational tempo have increased. For each serviceman there are two behind him. The second is recovering and a man is in retraining. In the year 2000 the military's budget has continued to decrease during the past eight years. The services are forced a way to book the cost of the numerous facets of military life. In summary the military serviceman is coupled with little money, which leads to low morale and poor training.

FACT# 2: Military deployments have increased dramatically during the 1990s.

The pace of deployments has increased tenfold since the end of the Cold War. Between 1960 and 1971, the Army conducted ten operations outside of normal operations. Between 1992 and 1998, it conducted 26 tasks. The Marines conducted 15 operations from 1982 to 1989 and 62 missions in 1989. During 2,000 or more troops, they were engaged in non-war fighting missions in the Middle East. General Henry Shelton quoted that the Army has 144,716 soldiers in 126 countries.

This dramatic increase of use of the Armed Forces has a detrimental effect on readiness. People and equipment wear out faster compared with frequent use. According to the Congressional Budget Office (CBO), a survey of Army Units that endorsed peacetime missions, the majority said 2/3 admitted that their individual preparations had declined. Training is the key to success and readiness. Operational Allied Force caused 22 exercises to be aborted. Another case of inadequate training was exposed in the Air Force. Airborne warning and control systems (AWACS) crews suffered 13 out of 40 AWACS crews were inadequately trained. Thus the rest of the remaining crews carried the load of all mission tasks. This was also uncalled for as the U-2 pilots were equally as bad.

The stress of frequent and unexpected deployment to the moral and jeopardizes the Armed Forces to retain high-quality men and women. Many men are married which leaves a strain on family life. This does cause an effort that may lead to leaving the service.

Between 1991 and 1994, the percentage of mission-capable Air Force fighter aircraft has decreased from 85% to 75%. The higher-ups in the Pentagon state that the average age is 20 years; however, the aircraft last only 15 years of life. The US Air Force has an inventory of B-52's, B-1's, and B'2's aircraft. The Air Force claims the next bomber will be in 2037. The B-52 will be 90 years old by the time the new bomber rolls out of the hangar! The Navy, however, has cut and the ships have begun to age rapidly. Amphibious ships are twenty-two years old. The Navy has forced to cut ship-building accounts from 8.7 per year, the number needed to maintain a 300-ship Navy to 65 ships per year.

FACT# 4: Morale is on the decline in the U.S. Armed Forces.

The military life is the "quality of life paid by lip service." Poor living conditions impair all military servicemen. The pay is lousy, but then work is underestimated with lack of essential parts to fix operation aircraft, ships, or vehicles.

Another problem is pay for the enlisted serviceman. The current pay (2000) is the current pay gap of 13%. This is complainant with the dissatisfied with what they are doing or in other words, let's move on to better things. In other words let's retire. There is more opportunity on the outside. Really?

The military's greatest asset is its quality of men, well trained, and can handle any task. The Army and the Air Force fell short of the 1999 recruiting goals—6,017, 1,700, respectively. The Navy also fell short because 7,000 sailors are locked in 1998. The Marines were short on repairing for Bradley type vehicles. So morale troubles military readiness and low morale is a red indicator of the U.S. military declining readiness.

In conclusion, the year 2000 shows a neglect of misdirected plans which, with a myopic strategy, have seen a decorated view that there has rendered American top forces below top form.

The recent casualties of high command, i.e., CIA Director (formerly Afghanistan commander) David Petraeus, General Carter F. Horn (AFICOM), and Admiral Charles M. Gaouette (Carrier Task Force Stennis) were the commander-in-chief purge that was affected in September after the Benghazi attack in 2012. General William "Kip" Ward (former AFRICACOM) lost or was stripped of a star plus Afghanistan Marine General John R. Allen was involved in a scandal, a sex scandal with Petraeus. This coincides with the purge of Stalin's/Hitler top military men that do not "toe the line."

Petraeus was either sacked or was a victim of something that was in error. He thought the attack was a result of an amateurish video calling Mohamed a pedophile and a self-proclaimed murder. In other words, a sex scandal was incorporated or to keep his mouth shut!

The dismissal of Ham where reports of him having assets in place set to rescue Ambassador Chis Smith and his team. Much to Ham's discussion, his team was ordered to stand down!

In a highly unusual move, Gaoutte bit the bullet and was relieved after deploying advance forces into the Libyan area. Rear Admiral Charles M. Gaouette was relieved from command of his powerful Carrier Strike Group Three (CSG 3), which was then located in the Middle East. CSG 3 is one of five located or assigned to the U.S. Pacific Fleet. Its missions are employed in various roles, such as gaining and maintaining sea control or projecting power onshore while projecting naval air both at sea and onshore. USS *Stennis* (CNN-74) has other units assigned, which include guided-missile cruisers and guided-missile destroyers.

Treason, General Ham Command of Africa Operations, relieved of duty for trying to save us in Benghazi; Rear Admiral Gaouette of the Mideast carrier group likewise relieved of command.

The reports show Obama's represented firing of a powerful U.S. Navy Admiral during a crisis time threat, Admiral Gaouette's removal was due to inappropriate leadership judgment. This report states the admiral's firing by President Obama was due to this strike force commander disobeying orders when he moved his forces on September 11, 2012, to assist American military forces ordered into action by the U.S. Army General Carter Ham, the Commander of the United States African Command (AFRICOM). The primary reason for this action was terrorist forces attacking American Consulate in Benghazi, Libya.

General Ham was in command during the 2011 U.S. NATO military involved in one country in the affairs of another in Libya. General Ham, like Admiral Gaouette, was also fired by Obama! And as far as we can tell, there is a growing sharp disagreement between the White House and U.S. military leaders.

General Ham received the emails that the White House got requesting help/support while the attack was taking place. General Ham immediately got a rapid force organized and advised he had a force ready. Ham obtained the order to stand down. His response was to screw it, but within 30 seconds or a minute when down, his second-in-command saw General Ham and told him he was now relieved of command! U.S. Air Force Jet Fighters were sitting on the tarmac 450 miles in Aviona, Italy, within 90 minutes from Benghazi. Yes, the commander-in-chief lied!

An organization has been started by our Armed Forces to get out the vote in 2014. This can be done by all of us. The president, the commander-in-chief, has made the Rules of Engagement (ROE) so difficult that our troops are often killed before they can get permission to fight. Nothing has been done to stop our troops from being murdered by Afghanis they are training. Now, the president wants the United States to sign on to the United Nations International Criminal Court (ICC), which would allow them to arrest and try U.S. troops for war crimes. This would be done without the legal protections guaranteed under U.S. law and which there is no appeal. The president, with his "Democratic" control of the Senate, has almost all the power. If the non-establishment can take back the Senate in 2014, our troops can once more be protected from unnecessary danger.

George W. Bush was president when you heard about the military deaths and Iraq, and Afghanistan daily. With Obama in the White House, the major trend of the media was quiet. More than 1,000 American soldiers have lost their lives in Afghanistan in the last 27 months. This reaches more than the combined total of the nine years before. During the last month, over 50 additional NATO and U.S. servicemen have been murdered. It is believed that who are hired is to be a force for good in Afghanistan.

The commander-in-chief is absent without leave! Not a peep, although he ordered the White House flag flown at half staff for the Shiites who were killed. There is a deep rumble, a fury, growing in the ranks of our military against the incompetence of this commander-in-chief.

No one knows what to do about the president, but the anger runs deep with no foolish end to the idiocy of this war. Obama has had four years to end this mentally ill during which time he has vacationed, golfed, campaigned, and generally ignored our men and women in uniform. Now, a movement afoot in the Armed Services to launch a massive get-out vote against this man. There is for active-duty types, National Guard, Reserves, the retired, and all other prior service members. This is no small special interest group, but many millions of veterans will have an enormous impact of the November 2014 election.

In Florida alone, it could mean an overwhelming victory if they all showed up at the polls. It might not keep another 100 U.S. troops from dying between now and November. This heartbreaking lack of leadership can make a powerful statement that more swiftly to change the indifference of this little man who just lets our soldiers die.

The assault on the United States continues at full force. The long term of Obama's remaining three years has always been to tear down the strength of our military power, and they are doing this despite when China, Russia, Iran, and al Qaeda ability to down was accelerating. Below in the article you can figure out how the commander-in-chief continues his assault on military personnel. They have repeatedly put the lives on the line and many have been maimed for life. The deepest and sometimes draconian cuts lie in the pay and benefits, which are proposed in the new budget. It includes:

(1) Increasing health costs for military families and retirees.
(2) Massive cuts in commissary benefits – cost of food will be increased.
(3) Cutting basic housing for families
(4) Pay raises in 2015 will be 1%, won't keep up with inflation
(5) U.S. Army shall reduce below 1940 levels costs, which is an extremely dangerous situation and relates to weakness.
(6) The Secretary of Defense relates there is, without a doubt, some risk involved.

There is serious study in the U.S. Armed Forces are getting or how many are getting food stamps because of their unusually low incomes. Because their pay is cut, the Obama Administration provides free medical care, education, and stamp benefits for illegal immigrants. Not to muddle the waters, the IRS has billions of dollars in employers paid federal taxes and also those who file for Illegal children residing in Mexico!

Annually the Obama Administration has increased food stamps (48 million) on food stamps, which exceeds the authorized allotment for the defense of our country. To think highly about issues is not common in the Obama Administration. To prevent war, we must build a vibrant, strategic military structure that creates "Peace Through Strength" and not peace through weakness.

The Department of Defense (DOD) and after weeks of delay with the Pentagon are finally ready to the DOD budget starting in 2016. $535 billion budget in one instance is $36 billion over the sequester cap. Inevitably the offset of defense increase will help solve the problem.

Senior White House officials say that they are resisting the largest reductions, including a Navy plan to cut an aircraft carrier and ramp down the manpower cuts. These cuts are serious whereby the money would mysteriously come from to pay for the items that have to be cut 2015. Another trick in the bag is the "wish list" from each branch of service.

At the highest lists of cuts, the officials were without a doubt surprised by the depth and reach of surprise when the Navy's aircraft carriers (11) would be eliminated. When the details are hammered out the budget roughly is $396 billion.

Rear Admiral John Kirby said the DOD 2015 budget will remain under caps mandated by the budget deal. Constructed by Senator Patty Murray (D-Wash) and Republican Paul Ryan (R-Wis) worked out a deal with $30 billion will land in the Pentagon safe!

The Navy's plan will do away with the Japan-based carrier George Washington (GW) and one of the 10 carrier air wings received lawmakers' attention. The GW, a 22-year-old vessel, is to undertake $3.9 billion and a refueling, overall which will keep it turning for another 23 years. The Navy commences to focus on the carrier and aircraft as a way to reduce spending and promote money for other ships, namely submarines and amphibious ships. Personnel billets would be cut 5,000 seagoing billets. Let's leave this for another year, not one in a political year 2014!

No ships are true and the red, white, and blue of America power. The White House has rescinded its response to tear down a carrier. There is another problem: no funding or proceed with the nuclear refueling overhaul much less operate it upon return to battleship status.

The Navy has received $ 245 million in procurement, but as yet it lacks $491 million for 2015. Even 2016 and 2017 looks bleak in order to complete GW's overhaul. This goes on fiscal year after year leaving next year—we hope!

President Obama is seeking to abolish the highly successful missile program, which is without a military superiority, a plague for our security by 2016. The Tomahawk program is the best of the best missiles acquired by the U.S.; however, it would drop to 2015 and the number equates to zero in 2016. This most advanced missile is set to be cut by $128 million under Obama's fiscal year 2015 and would be eliminated in 2016. Also the Navy will be forced to drop its highly effective Hellfire missiles. Erosion, lack of firepower, and shock to lawmakers cause a definite ability to deter enemy invasions.

This dangerous void is left with gaps in key areas. The U.S. Navy depended on them, i.e., Benghazi in 2011 and some 200 Tomahawks were employed during this fight. 100 per year are used on an average, meaning drastic cuts will be made throughout 2018. The Navy has used this missile during Desert Strom and battle zones from Iraq, Afghanistan to the Balkans. With budget scaling back production, this missile must be funded.

Navy experts predict the loss of these missile systems will jeopardize its supremacy of power as it faces North Korea to the Middle East. Lieutenant Colonel Steve Russell, who is running for Congress, says that if we are not replacing them, what are we in heaven's name going to do? North Korea has fired several missiles, including ballistic missiles. Possibly the Navy's defensive stand will become more important in the Pacific in years to come.

Chief of Naval Operations (CNO) Admiral Jonathon Greenert was visiting Naval Station Mayport, Florida, and has stated that there was no need to go through base closures. The Defense Report has requested Congress approve another round of Base Closure and Realignment (BRAC). This plan was to take effect or begin in 2017.

In visiting Mayport the CNO took exception with BRAC, as he feels there are no cuts necessary for this installation. The East Coast is proud that its communities are virtually dependent on military spending both construction and everyday living. We need another BRAC like a "hole in the head"! Money for this infrastructure is close, but Congress can't allow this military strategic base to close. Even in the Hampton Roads area, there are two fine military, Naval Station Norfolk, VA, for example, maintaining multiple ships, submarines, and carriers. The balance of powers are one in the East- submarines in Groton, CT, and the balance of power lies in Mayport and in Norfolk, VA. The 2005 BRAC almost made major adjustment when it nearly happened to a Navy jet base in Virginia Beach, VA. All of the leaders are coming together.

A wartime high 570,000 troops but the slimming down of 530,00 to 490,000 a goal that could or should be at the end of 2015. The rule for the Army is, how can its force exist on 490,000? Think about 2016. Lieutenant General James Barclay cautioned that we do not fall to 420,000. Many decision points must fall into place. One thing is clear, not too many budgeters are believing the changes are due, which will be submitted in less than a month.

Defense Secretary Hagel announced a new budget (2015) that he acknowledged was a bit too controversial, yet it blended in with the Afghanistan and the Iraq wars. Here is a sample of these hellacious cuts:

- These are the right thing to do during war.
- This is the budget that's not war-based effort.
- It cuts out the growth of housing and commissaries will be reduced.
- Only the retired will escape proposed cuts to co-pays and increases to deductions.
- Pay raises will be 1% in 2015; general and flag will seek a pay freeze.
- A new round of base closings.
- Army reduced to 520,000 to 440,000 or 450,000.

- Army National Guard to 350,000 to 335,000; Army reserve 205,000 to 335,000.
- The Marine Corps from 190,000 to 182,000.
- He surmised a smaller ground force would still defeat an enemy with air and naval forces.
- Pentagon proposed to cut programs not geared for future wars.
- Eliminate Air Force A-10 Warthog $3.5 billion over the next five years.
- Retire the U-2 program and replace it with the Global Hawk drone.
- This budget cut the Navy combat ships from 52 to 32.

The elimination of the A-10 will be an argumentative issue. Senator Kelly Ayotte (R-NH) said it was a serious mistake. The Defense is protecting it because it would cost lives. None the less, the investment of $26 billion will be used for readiness and modernization.

The 2015 budget falls within the $496 billion cap as suggested and for the next five years the ceiling will exceed $115 billion. If all this is done, Pentagon officials imply deeper cuts will be made, for example, the Army's duty size will be 420,000.

An organization action has been started by our own armed forces, to vote in 2014. This must be done by all of us. The president, the commander-in-chief, has invented Rules of Engagement (ROE) so strict that our troops are killed before they get permission to do battle! Our troops are being murdered by the Afghanis as they are training. Now the president wants the U.S. to sign on the United Nations International Criminal Court (ICC), which would allow to arrest and try U.S. soldiers for War Crimes. This would be done when legal protections guaranteed by the U.S. law, and from which there is no appeal. The president has almost all the power. If we can take back control of the Senate in 2014, our troops can once again be protected.

When George W. Bush was president, you heard of deaths of Iraq and Afghanistan daily. With Obama in the White House, the major trend of the media has been quiet! 1,000 soldiers lost their lives in Afghanistan during the past 27 months. This reaches a combined total of nine years before. During the past month, 50 NATO and U.S. serviceman have been wiped away. The president (CIC) is absent without leave! Not a peep, although he permitted the White House flag at half mast because the Sikhs that were decimated. There is a deep rumble of fury growing in the ranks of the military against the incompetence of this commander-in-chief.

No one knows what to do about him, but the anger runs deep with no foolish end in sight. Three more years to end this mentally ill, during time you name it, vacationed, golfed, campaigned, and generally blew off the plight of our courageous men and women in uniform.

Now a movement afloat in which the armed service to get out and vote against this president. This is for the active duty, National Guard, Reserves, the retired and he remaining prior members. This is no small group but millions of veterans will have a tremendous impact on the outcome of the November 2014 election.

In Florida alone can never an overwhelming victory in that state. One hundred dying U.S. troops will not stop this spirited rage! This heartbreaking lack of leadership will make a powerful edge that more swiftly to change the indifference of this little man who lets our soldiers die!

"Readiness, moderation, capability: Those are priorities that we focus on. As you assess your resources and you match your resources to mission, those are three priorities that always must be in front of everything else" (U.S. Defense Secretary Chuck Hagel).

CHAPTER 9

DEPARTMENT OF HOMELAND SECURITY

The Department of Homeland Security (DHS) is a department of the federal government. It has the primary responsibility of protecting the United States and its territories from/or land, manmade accidents, and natural disasters. The DHS and the Department of Interior is equal with respect to Interior ministries of other countries.

While the Department of Defense is responsible for all military actions abroad the DHS works with civilians to protect the United States within, at, or outside its border. Its goal is to protect, prepare for, prevent, and respond to domestic emergencies, in fact all acts of terrorism. In March 2013 DHS took on the Immigration and Naturalization Service (INS). Upon knowing this major task, it divided this into two separate organizations: Immigration and Customs Enforcement and the Citizen and Immigration Service. This was only the beginning as they were transformed into the Homeland Security Investigations. The INS was broken down into the U.S. Border Patrol, U.S. Customs Service, and Animal and Plant Health Inspection Service. Finally, the U.S. Customs and Border Protection gave birth.

We are 200,000 employees as DHS is the third-largest cabinet department. Coordination of Homeland Security Policy is done at the Whitehouse by the Homeland Security council. On December 16, 2013, Jeb Johnson was appointed as next Secretary of Homeland Security.

On September 11, 2001, President George W. Bush announced the establishment of the Office of Homeland Security. He appointed Governor Tom Ridge as leader of DHS. Under Ridge's plan he stripped 180,000 government employees their Union rights, and President Bush signed into law the Homeland Security Act of 2002 on November 25, 2002. By far was the largest group of manpower ever envisioned in fifty years.

On March 12, 2002, the Homeland Security Advisory System produced a color-coded terrorism risk was a result of the Presidential Directive. This program was to effective means to disseminate information to all major states and especially to the American people. The plan, although caused many slip-ups, was altered to the National Terrorism Advisory System (NTAS) within the United States. Another program is called the *Ready.gov*, a readiness website. The conception of this relies on the launch of the Iraq war. Chemical attack was the victim and the use of duct tape and protective sheeting led to building a homemade bunker. Fortunately, the price of these two parcels went over the high time sales – could be an alarmist possibility?

Many critics have dogged the HDS official and stuff about the excessive waste and downright lack of transparency. The House of Representatives Sub Committee on September 8, 2008, stated that the Department squandered $15 billion in failed contracts. Many contracts, as noted by the Government Accountability Office, revealed that purchases of beer brewing kits unusable plastic "dog booties," in boats purchased at double the price. The boats now purchased now could not be found!

Between 2003 and 2008 a long line of Fusion Centers coupled with DHS reports contains a wide strip of data, which could be used as a threat to national protection. All sorts of indicators are popping up that labels Muslim hacks are a danger, other samples are in Wisconsin where anti-abortion activities are troubled and at best are used in troubled areas in Pennsylvania, the Tea Party, and in Maryland State Police put a defender, anti-war persons in the Federal Terrorism database.

Another gaff is the spending measure approved would pull the bottle on funding for a new HDS in Southeast Washington, D.C. This provision lacked 200 million dollars less than was requested in 2014. This approach is sponsored by the Republicans, who describes its bill as "responsible choices" to save tax-payer dollars by lowering overhead costs and reducing funding for lower fund-ing programs.

Eleven years old and the third-largest segment in the Federal govern-ment, it operates with 50 facilities throughout the Washington region. The overhaul contribution began in 2008 but the final phase has begun without the Coast Guard Headquarters opening last July. The program has run into major deficiencies saying the program is running ten years behind schedule. Construction delays among other problems, the cost have skyrocketed with a total one billion dollars short of original estimates.

Another pain-in-the-ass is the happening in America—and it's not a step toward liberty. In an alarming memo that shocked Mr. Hagmann was a direc-tive agreed upon by the DHS chief Janet Napolitano and the head of the

Transportation Security Administration (TSA) John Pistole. The memo by Doug Hagmann was to be aware of those engaged in the new airport screening procedures as domestic extremists. The terminology expressed in the memo is indeed troubling. The memo labels anyone who objects with TSA airport security procedures is against established screening format will be called a domestic extremist. This must be widened so that if one objects to, helps, and supports for anyone who engages in travel to break apart at U.S. airports to enhance security.

The recent inquiry of appropriation of weapons by the Department of Homeland Security can mean that it's a cry to a threat of war by this administration. The DHS has been holding back in order to provide to you, citizens of America, the recent purchase of weapons of mass destruction! They purchased 3,000 mine-resistant ambush-protected (MRAP) armor-protected personnel carriers. This includes 1.6 billion rounds of ammunition along with competitive weapons. This weapon buying, the DHS has no authority to plan/initiate war missions or planning within the United States. Significant is the fact that the Commander in Chief is arming for was within the confidence of the USA in accordance with his 2008 campaign oratory. "We've gotta have a national security force that's just as strong, just as well funded as the United States Military." The Obama Administration is defending, overextending, and has a cavity inside the Department of Defense – the only agency with a war mission.

Our president stands as a glaring threat of war against our citizens. This act is an unresolved problem, the peace-loving citizens are left to defend themselves against the administration "coup" against the people and the crowd will fight for liberty defended for 238 years!

The proper response is to gear up the House and Senate to demand that the Homeland Security immediately surrender their weapons of destruction to the Department of Defense. The tyrannical acts to exercise its limiting power establishes by our founding fathers, to destroy the DHS as soon as available. One has to look at Adolf Hitler and his associated DHS take control over the German public. It does not seem likely in 2014 to see a Marxist Obama Administration make such a person power grab!

For more than two centuries this country has lived in peace due to our strong military. Should we have the same proponents against a "domestic" enemy? Our constitution does not include an overthrow by a rogue agent pertaining to Marxist leadership. We will not surrender ourselves as easy prey to leaders that will ruin our nation!

Another version of Homeland Security is when a Captain Terry Hestilow wrote a letter to his local senator, The Honorable Senator John Cornyn, from the State of Texas. He says that the recent appropriation of weapons by the

Department of Homeland Security can only be a bold example of war by the agency, to the President of the United States and against the citizens of this country. DHS has been wonderful concerning of taking 3,000 mine resistant ambush protected (MRAP) armored carriers, 1.6 billion ammunition and other weapons. In fact, the DHS has no mission, for example, war mission or any task whereby there is no authority even to do this in the United States!

Significant, however, is the Obama Administration beefing up his DHS against the limits of war against the people of our country with agreement with his 2008 campaign speech. Thus the Obama management is defunding, overextending, and shutting down the DHS, the only agency of the United States with a open-armed conflict as its mission!

The art of Obama's government is a glaring threat of war against our nation's populace. Thus the "coup" against their liberty is fought for and defended the last 238 years. We have no other way if we honor our oaths and our dignity. Therefore, the Department of Homeland Security must immediately surrender their weapons of war to the Department of Defense.

One of the responsibilities is to provide facts on issues in order for the American citizens will be provided with the truth on problems with Obama. This provides coverage of the facts and are laid out on our New Rules of Engagement for our U.S. Border Patrol safety.

Homeland Security Officer Jeh Johnson was the first African-American who headed the DHS. This new code gives a self-defense from rock throwers. This act will reduce Mexicans from illegal entry across the United States border. Obama agrees with this policy but desires more lenient policing in dealing with the U.S./Mexican border. Police Executive Research Forum set forth that lawless is displayed by the Illegal aliens and puts more patrolmen in danger. This also doesn't have patrolman stand in front of vehicles for fear of being hit by rocks. Numerous Border Patrolman have put men in the hospital with critical injuries. Three patrolmen were shot with an AK-47 assault weapon that was provided by agents of the Obama Administration. Eric Holder is responsible for Fast and Furious gas smuggling program. The Border Patrol has been attacked 6,000 times since 2007 and assaulted repeatedly with large rocks.

Obama's newly appointed Homeland Security has turned the procedure. Johnson reacted against opposition from the Veteran Border Patrolmen, and on his first day of the job he forced Federal law which caused more lives in danger. This new law encourages drug cartels and human cartels in Mexico to become more active. Speaker Boehner has to take action because the lives of Federal Law Enforcement Officers are in jeopardy.

Obama is kindling the fire because he did to the U.S. Combat troops in Afghanistan, forcing dangerous Rules of Engagement on them (personnel killed in action by casualties 458%). The Speaker of the House must take action against the Mexicans against preventing them from defending or telling him to run. For 17 months the Speaker has failed to establish a Select House Investigative Committee with subpoena authority on Benghazi. These should be a change within the House!

For more than multiple centuries we have peace throughout our nation because of our legitimate military. We must stand up for freedom and not let this overthrow democracy and to implement legal steps to amend our grievances. The Department of Homeland Security has recently turned in to a national police force. Looking back on the increased military backup, this has evolved into "a standing army on American soil." DHS has with 240,000 full-time employees with many agencies under them, has been known as a galloping train! A better plan is to abolish this third-largest federal agency. Every deed, tactic, or sugar-coated policy can be traced to the DHS mindset of the police state, and billions of dollars goes to grants permits by police agencies.

These are some of the agencies that they endorse:

- Militarizing Police and SWAT Teams: Purchase military vehicle, etc.
- Spying on Unknown Activists, Dissents, and Veterans.
- Stockpiling Large Amounts of Ammunition: DHS has 260 million rounds of ammunition, which relates to approximately 15,000 rounds per officer.
- Distribution of license plate to identify cars, check their database, and track them.
- Tracking cell phones.
- Military Drills and lockdowns in USA cities.
- Using TSA as an early warning device.
V• IPR Task Forces: Comprised of air marshals, security inspectors, and detection/explosive teams that have mobilized the "soft" targets such as stadiums, malls, etc.
- Conducting Widespread Spying Using Fusion Control Centers.
- Carrying Out Border Searches
- Promoting and Funding Surveillance of City Cameras
- Drone Use

It is without a mystery that DHS is known for its "wasteful, growing, fear-mongering beast."

CHAPTER 10

LET'S REVISIT OBAMA'S BIRTH CERTIFICATE

The "birther" is a subject that records a definition beyond any person that may be born outside of the United States of America who can legally declare he or she is qualified to be President of the United States. Realistically, this implies that President Barack Obama was not born in this country, USA, that is. So how can one believe that he can validate his citizenship, or can he prove that he was born in Hawaii? Actually he was brought forth in the moment of birth in Mombaso, Kenya, and his mother knows that since she was there!

On June 27, 2004, a Kenyan paper published an innocent story about a native son was moving upward to success. Barack Obama was his name and the story was not a birther article. This was a simple story about a man who was making good as a Kenyan-born man. This story has been removed and a cover-up is not out of question.

If you read the article, the "AP" appears at the end. The Associated Press wrote 90% of the press release and The Standard added Obama was born in Kenya. This piece of data simply says that the Associated Press did not write 100% of this story, but this is not credible. If this does not prove that Barack Obama was born in Kenya, then one would seriously investigate this event. Of all newspapers in America and book publishers states that Obama was born in Kenya long before he ran for president. Funny, people won't even listen or believe that logic!

It was evident that in a Kenyan newspaper, *Sunday Standard* indicating Kenyan born, all set for the Senate the Nigerian Observer advertised in November 2008 that the Kenyan born Senator was a scooped candidate to run the United States Presidential race. Obviously there were many papers that supported him that say that he was Kenyan born.

Thus the financial fact that numerous documents were missing or had been removed were documented. The State of Hawaii had denied or refused multiple pleas including Maricopa, Arizona county Sheriff's Office posse to pre-pare or release an original long space form birth certificate. Many flaws were in-dicated in the official birth notices released by the White House. The reason that Obama is to believe his father's Kenya and British citizenship denies natural-born status, thus data precludes Obama from serving as president. Obama was certainly born in Kenya and it is certain that Michelle Obama once called Kenya his "home country." An investigation team as discovered records from the U.S. National Archives that were missing. *Breitbart.com* released Obama's authorized biography, which was from his itinerary agent in 1991 and says he was born in Kenya. This written bio reminds the same through reprinting in 2007.

The social number released in Connecticut in 1972 or 1977 has never claimed he lived there or held a job there. His first job was in Hawaii at Baskin Robbins. This is a number of 16 or so numbers that have been linked to Obama and his aliases.

The British National Archives (BNA) is an executive of the government of the United Kingdom based in Kew southwest on London. The BNA has 1,000 years of history with records of parchment and numerous paper scrolls and paper files. These represent the Foreign Office and Colonial Office. This collection is held by BNA and may be searched using their Archives is free of charge.

Destroyed files were recovered recently and the "lost" colonial-era files on the former colony of Kenya. They found that Obama Senior, the father of the President of the United States (POS), is top of the list revealed a British listing of Kenyan's studying in the United States.

The unusualness of this event is forthcoming! In May 2012 someone con-ducting a search and found an unnamed son of Obama Senior was born in Kenya in 1961. POS living in the White House is the only known child of Obama Senior after 1960. It is true that Kenya became officially an independ-ent from the UK, and it is reasonable to conclude that the President of the United States is the unnamed child of Obama Senior, born in Kenya in 1961, his mother Stanley Ann Durham. Preciously the claimed birth date of Barack Obama is August 4, 1961.

The newest theory that cements Obama is the bold evidence that he will annul the presidency of the United States. Occidental College proves that his college transcripts regarding application and receiving foreign student aid ver-ified this. Under the name "Barry Soetoro," he applied for aid and was awarded a scholarship from the Fulbright Foundation Scholarship Program. To get a half loaf of bread, he furthermore had to prove foreign scholarship. This ho-listic purge is the smoking gun that many distractions have been searching for.

Amazing volume of records illustrates Obama legally registered as Barry Soetoro. School records show this name and this is recorded at Occidental

College. He is also listed as a foreign student, not an American citizen. This would erupt a weapon of mass destruction if he is from and born in Indonesia! The first name of a child is the same from birth. To enlist a child for school his official birth certificate is required. All of the evidence has been received, Barack Obama first name, legal first name, is Barry not Barrack!

A biography picture of Obama's Occidental College days states he is 18 or 19 years old and attended this school as Barry Soetoro. His first name was changed by a girl, Regina, who started to call him Barack. There is no reason or no record of his name change.

While being sworn as an attorney in the state of Illinois, he responded not at all to the use of other names. Mr. Soetoro/Obama clearly defrauded the State Bar of Illinois and perjured himself while hiding his identity. More importantly, why did he conceal his falsehood?

Registration transcripts states: Name – Barry Soetoro –
Religion: Islam – Nationality: Indonesian.

91

The evidence is adequate to eliminate this person, Barack Obama, as the President of the United States. Official Occidental College documents/transcripts registered and stamped with state approval declares Obama is an imposter!

The United States Constitution specified that the president or vice president must be natural-born citizens. Obama has not or definitely not met the standard. In fact, there are numerous lawsuits that are not eligible for commander-in-chief, president, or in fact, this is a felonist fraud! In fact, soldiers have challenged his illegitimacy on federal lawsuits.

One such soldier was a U.S. Army Major Stefan Frederick Cook, who was given orders to deploy to Afghanistan. He appeared these orders by stating that Obama is not a U.S. Citizen, thereby he has no authority to be president and commander-in-chief. The military revoked the orders (no specific reason given) and this would not go to court before a judge! In a twenty-page document – U.S. District Court for the Middle District of Georgia – the California-based Taitz asks the court to consider his belief that Obama is not a natural-born citizen of the U.S. and is not eligible to serve as commander-in-chief, the *Ledger – Engineer* reported.

In complete knowledge of all of the false actions that have come to the surface this birther nonsense is absurd. No intelligent-thinking individual could ever doubt that Obama was not born in Hawaii.

On January 24, 2011, a former elections clerk, Tim Adams, swearing the affidavit he signed in Hawaii that no long form was generated at a hospital for Barack Obama. Related to this signed affidavit was never Queens Medical Center or Kapi/Olani Medical in Honolulu had no record of his birth in either hospital.

Adams was employed by the city and the Honolulu Electronics Division from May 2008 to September 2009. He was a Senior Elections Clerk, overseeing 60 employs which verified the identity of voters and the absentee ballot box. Adams became aware of the need to obtain the long form document. His employees backed him when he announced that no record was ever recorded in the Hawaii Department of Health. Adams later told the World Net Daily (WND) that repeat no long form Hospital generated could be found at the Hawaii Department of Health.

In 2009 WND reported that Obama has changed his birth site from Queens Medical to Kapi/Olini Medical Center with a certain mystery explaining the connection. Another scoop was when Governor Neil Abercrombie became involved in a birth controversy when he read a letter suspiciously authored by President Obama saying that Kapi/Olani was his birth hospital. The White House neither said it wrote or sent the statement in the letter. The affidavit squares that during my course of employment we included notary names of government officials in Hawaii that no official could find evidence that a long form birth certificate for Senator Obama had been issued from Hawaii hospitals at the time of birth. The short spaced form certification of birth is not significant proof that Obama was born in Hawaii. My basic assumption is that he was not born here (Adam said).

With multiple piles of copies of Barack Hussain Obama, "real" birth certificates, many are revealing clearly a fraud. With an explosive reaction the Alabama Supreme Court has entered a bodacious birth notification that is different from the one posted in the web site 2011 in the White House.

Larry Klayman, acting as the plaintiff's counsel, submitted a fake of Obama's birth notice that was posted April 7, 2001. Anything the group submitted still is a bogus one and yet a third sample was presented by the Alabama Democrats to the Supreme Court. This court was being presided by the Chief Justice Moore who supported Lieutenant Colonel Terry Lake when he believed Obama was a usurper. He also denied him from deploying to Iraq. Tom Parker, another Justice on the Court, will also hear the trial. He said that McInnish has attached certain legal proof that the appropriate form gave the evidencury presentation , would raise certain questions about the authenticity of the "short form" and the "long form" certificates that President Barack Hussein Obama had made public.

While the Obama Democrats attacked the actions of this appeal but states a country Sheriff from Arizona is not subject to official source of anything in the great state of Alabama. What stands out is the long form birth certificate has a different banding! There are hundreds of layers according to Adobe expert Mara Zebest. He said that the document displays a permutation of the birth that should not come as a surprise. Current variation proves the layers displayed in the White House and PDF of official birth are a "big fucking deal" to quote Joe Biden. This variation proves the manipulation creates Obama's PDF that due to layers, it's easy for such to happen. Notice there is no raised seal which must be on the document to make it official.

The birth report was e filed by the Alabama Democratic Party, but notice the e-filing did not have the diamond pattern or the subject e-filing. Also, pixel patriot demonstrated that security paper background extended beyond the right side further that the visible area of PDF copy.

This malicious lie is living out Democratic left and right when they are openly procreating a man in the Oval Office. It appears that we have a man in the White House that we cannot say he is from this country and must be providing cover up, what should be the biggest story in America! Obama's eligibility issue is no doubt bigger than scandals which tear down tentacles around things that destroys. In other words, a "birther" issue, it's not. It's not a criminal issue, it's not a national security issue.

From another issue that this birth certificate is a forgery, many think, or rather truth, that he is listed as white or he is not a bona fide or United States citizen. In April 2011, the President sought to dispel rumors concerning his citizenship that he released a long copy that proved that this document was true beyond a shadow of a doubt!

The Hawaii Department of Health complied with certified copies of a live birth defined as a "long form" birth certificate.

Loretta Fuddy (the Hawaii Health Director) attested and verified the certified to the president further proved he was born in Hawaii.

April 25, 2011, pursuant to Obama's request, Director Fuddy personally saw the copying of the original document of Live Birth and with her hands on the Holy Bible presented this to the Doctor Aluin Onaka, the Hawaii State Register.

CERTIFICATE OF LIVE BIRTH

As with the same piece of 2008, the birthers made known that the paper displayed erroneous factors. Paramount was the textual principles that were anachronistic. Secondly, the Adobe illustrator, you guessed it, had been altered! 64

Back in 1961 all people were called "Negroes," so how come the birth certificate claimed he was "African-American" when such a term was not produced at this time?

Obama's birth was listed as August 4, 1961, and listed his father's age as 25 years old born in Kenya, East Africa. Kenya did not exist as a state until 1963. How could Obama's father have been in a state that did not exist? This country was known as the "British East Africa Protectorate"!

The White House birth certificate revealed the place of birth is "Kapiolani Maternity and Gynecological Hospital." In 1961 the hospitals were known as "Kauli Keolani Children's Hospital" and "Kapi olani Materning Home." The name did not change the name in 1978. How can this goal exist particularly in view of the President of the United States! This claims to 1961 are not proper:

- Nowhere on Barack Obama's birth certificate does the statement "African-American" appear. The race of father is stated as "African," which at that time blacks were actually African. They never used "black or negro," which was characteristic of being a slave.

The British Empire in 1895 established the East Africa Protectorate. Kenya joined a state in 1963, two years before Obama's birth was announced in 1961.

Obama's Certificate of Birth

Barack Obama was not born in Kapi'olani Hospital or any such establishment.

A listing of social services in the Hawaii Islands states the facility that bore any names prior to 1961:

EXAMPLE

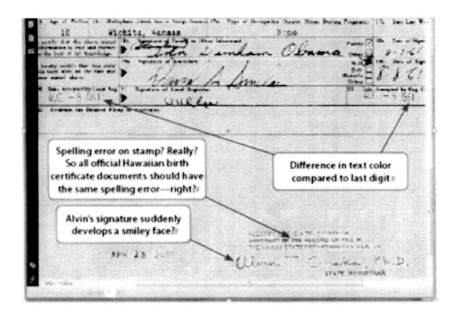

Obama's birth certificate, 4/27/11.
Inconsistencies in pixel colors and spelling errors.

Moreover, a copy of a birth certificate to a child born in Hawaii one day after Obama also shows in the "Name of Hospital," Kopi'oloni Maternity and Gynecological Hospital. The birth certificate PDF file of the Adobe Illustrator reveals multiple layers – the image was altered! It did not take long for the doubters the White House had altered or it might be assessed as a fake.

Adobe Illustrator has been a premier program for computer graphic experts – it reveals that nine separate layers have been analyzed . This document has claimed that it's proof that it has been violated.

An expert, Jean-Claude Tremblay, said that the evidence of common scanning software was not evidence of forgery. The leading software man does rite that scanning software will try to separate the text and the background into parts of and particularly layers. John Woodum also debunked the layers argument by a series of photos:

EXAMPLE

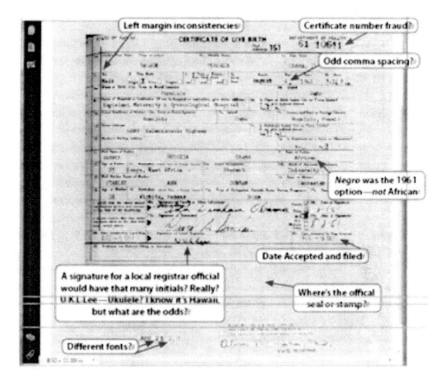

Obama's birth certificate, 4/27/11.
Overall information defies common sense.

The March "Cold Case Posse" produced by Arizona sheriff Joe Arpaio produced no evidence concerning a forgery, and in July 2012 more rumors had already been debunked! Dan Pfeiffer, a White House Communicator Director, put out an affirmative report of the Presidents long form birth certificate. In 2008 the President requested his birth announcement from Hawaii. The state sent the required certificate which is the same as if Hawaii's needed proof of birth.

When any citizen asks for an exact date of birth, this authorizes a driver's license and is legal for all Federal Government and the courts for all legal purposes. The president believes the distraction and disbelief over his birth document was not good for the country nor was it good for television! By his authority, he sought the long form and that Hawaii State Department of Health make an exception to do this: Hawaii granted this request.

Steve Stockman suspected that he would follow "birther" news. He was not afraid of these as he followed articles when they come out and are not holding back because you may be laughing at me!

News reported the Steve Stockmann was up support of a bill that eventually was against Obama ID Fraud Case. Who else would sponsor a bill? He among others would! The announcement came from Stockmann rather than Ted Yoho (FL-3rd District) who supports going on with the process.

Mr. Yohos endorsement was outstanding but hopefully it will follow his constituents wants. For a lot of Americans is what they have been waiting for 4 ½ years! It's in your court – write letters, call on the phone, send e-mails, and send faxes. Your local rep gets 5,000 commutations daily and do you expect he ignored them? We are tired of this fight – this is what we have been waiting for.

Loretta Fuddy was the Health Director that released a "Certificate of Live Birth" to the President. Fuddy died in a plane crash in 2013. The media narrative quickly fell apart. This article was published on December 12, 2013 and why birthers might opened the doors on this story.

The story released was that Loretta Fuddy prepared the release of the long-form Hawaii birth certificate. Of nine people on board that aircraft, she was the only one that died.

The *L.A. Times* reported the Cessna plane crashed, everyone was saved, yet Fuddy remained in the fuselage of the airplane! Two things surfaced when Terry Seelig told a falsehood:

1.   Fuddy held hands with Keith Yarmamoto in her final moments.

2.   We were under the impression that this plane would never be recovered.

Since her death there were significant reports on her financial reports declaring her income with expenses in 2011 and 2012. Yes, her tax reports show a $75,000 figure and paid $40,000 towards her mortgage which was more than she grossed that year. Yet she never disclosed this on financial forms she filled with the Hawaii State Ethics Commission.

Mr. Vogt brought some attention to this financial ruse one week before her death. Just one week before the airplane change? Let us summarize what we know is true:

1.   Hawaii government official swears the long-form birth certificate never existed.

2.   Loretta Fuddy produced a "Certificate of live birth."

3. Loretta Fuddy came to extra money, which she later applied to her mortgage.

4. Doug Vogt said Fuddy received extra money in a radio review.

5. A week later Loretta Fuddy is dead while the media screws up the story![66]

Obama's fake birth certificate is on the steps of the House of Representatives. Stockman is ready to kick the door in! An American since 1775 brings the fight against all odds; that's made this country great! Show Obama what we stand for, freedom and equality for all!

CHAPTER 11

THE GREATEST HOAX

O bama in 1960 happened to know various people. William Ayers, father Thomas Ayers, a close friend of Obama's communist mentor Frank Marshall Davis; friend of communist-sympathizing Chicago Vernon Jarrett; a father-in-law of Iranian-born Valerie Jarrett; and who Obama chose as his closest friend in the White House who managed to get millions of money from the Illinois legislation.

Valerie Jarrett worked for Chicago who happened to hire Michelle. La Vaughan Robinson (later Mrs. Obama) who worked at the Sidley Austin law firm. Barack Obama just happened to get a summer job there. Obama received a letter of recommendation from Percy Sutton who was a lawyer for Malcolm X, who was a close friend of Barack Hussein Obama Senior when Malcolm X traveled to Kenya. Obama Senior paid for his education at the University of Hawaii by putting up the money. The long line of donated bills wound up with the Nation of Islam, Louis Farraklan, who was located close to William Ayers and Bernardine Dohm to have been babysitters for the two Obama daughters.

Upon completion of Occidental and Columbia Universities (had Muslim roommates), he moved to Chicago where he worked for Industrial Areas Foundation which was founded by Marxist agitator Saul "the Red" Alinsky. As author of Rules for Radicals, and Obama salary of $25,000, this was provided by the Woods Fund where the Sarara Coal Company provided the black stuff to the Commonwealth Edison whose son William Ayers served on the board of Woods Fund, including Obama!

Obama worked on voter registration and became associated with the Democratic Socialists of America (DSA). He met Carl Davidson who had been to Vietnam to sabotage our own American effort. Davidson sponsored at 2002 anti-war rally where Obama spoke and later met Marilyn Katz who was a friend of Obama's hatchet man, David Axelrod.

Obama joined the Trinity United Church of Christ (TUCC) whose leader and minister is Reverend Jeremiah Wright who preached Marxism and Black Liberation Theology, that delivered anti-white, anti-Jew, or whatever. Obama never noticed that the church gave vile Islam teacher Louis Farrakhan a lifetime award!

Although no one noticed a $125,000 advance was given to Obama who used this money on vacation to Bali with his wife Michelle. $40,000 dollars later he wrote "Dreams From My Father," which amplified William Ayers who trampled on an America flag and was photographed in the popular Chicago magazine and appeared on the cover throughout the city.

Obama was hired by Miner, Banhill & Galland, and in 1994 he represented ACORN, which involved in banks being blackmailed for subprime loans, which among other tragic circumstances, led to the collapse of the housing bubble and helped Obama defeat the Republican in 2008.

In late 1999 Obama became engaged in homosexual and cocaine snorting in the backseat of a limousine with Larry Sinclair a gay director of Obama's Chicago church. In 2008 Sinclair was arrested because of a two murder charges based on a warrant issued by Delaware Attorney General Beau Biden!

In 2003 in honor of Rashid Khalidis who was a PLO operative, a loathe critic of Israel, and advocate of Palestinian rights, Obama and his wife attended a dinner. Obama continually praised Khalidi as he went to many dinners at which he funneled cash that Palestinians cannot get there land back, Israel "will never see a day of peace."

In 2004 Illinois Democratic primary race front runner Blair Hull was forced out of the race by Dave Axelrod got sealed divorce unsealed, which caused Obama to win the primary election. Obama waltzed into the Senate. After 143 days of work, he was certified to run for the President of the United States.[67]

On Sunday's show, September7, 2008, Senator Obama was asked by General Bill Gann, USAF (Ret) why he does he did not follow protocol when the National Anthem is played. According to the U.S. Code, during the playing of the National Anthem or when the flag is displayed, all are to stand at attention, facing the flag, and with their right hand over the heart.

Obama replied that the flag pin is a symbol of oppression. The anthem conducts a war-like cry through the air, for example, like bombs bursting in air. He then recommends that the National Anthem be the song, "I'd Like To Teach the World To Sing." Therefore, if elected I would disarm America to the level where Middle East Brethren would accept a Nation of warring people would conduct like Islam where peace prevails. Maybe a state of mutual accord can exist between our governments. We as a nation have placed on Islam, which is why my wife disrespects the flag and what it stands for in our country.

Now I have found myself about to become President of the United States and will put my hatred aside. I will use my power to change the nation and to offer a new way of life. My wife and I are looking to becoming the first black family. Change is about to overthrow this land know as the United States of America!

Steve Stockman is feared by the grocery stores because he voted against John Boehner for speaker. This is the man who exposed apambots in the anti-guns frecas. He among no others, knows of the entire legislation has interest in the Obama birth controversy.

Stockman is never afraid or has the stamapt to walking out of the State of the Union address and mention the "I" word. A Washington Times reports that Mr. Stockman said the President repeatedly broke his oath of office by supporting the Constitution and responding, he seriously is mulling appropriate action. This promoted filling Articles of Impeachment against President Obama as depicted on his website. Mr. Stockment said last year he considered taking legal action to stop Obama's fragrant abuse of power.

Recently the Government Accounting Office confirmed our growing national debt is, by and large, this very significant information has largely been denied by our national media. On the brink of a colossal monetary meltdown and the media is giving President Obama tips on how to destroy the Republican Party. If the American journalists permit a one party rule, plunk your magic dragon froggie, China and Russia their dreams come true!

President Obama reflects negatively has been discarded by most media people. The uncovering of the problems of Benghazi or the volatility of Africa and the problems of the Middle East, the national press refuses to ask the White House any serious questions. And did the Republicans really as bleary-eyed and dumb as they display? Believe the Hillary Clinton would come clean over the Benghazi cover up? Will she run for President in 2016 with 35 years misrepresenting the facts to her, repeat, her advantage. Are the Republications as bleary-eyed and as dumb as they display?

Believe it or not, the truth remains; America is headed down the drain if President Obama takes out his wallet! The stock market is making wealthy investors increasing their gains and taking advantage of The Federal Reserves by injecting millions of dollars in treasury notes with low interest rates. Republications and Democrats refuse to their sacred cows for the common good of the United States!

The political tightening and uncanny revolution, one can mount up into a civil war when the bank falls short and people will die. The fat cats will suffer and these people are no longer for the "reaper" will show no mercy! Eventually there should be a reasonable accountability and if the media detects it, the press will protect President Obama by telling the truth, as if he provokes to this day when no end in sight from 2008!

President Obama must change direction to solving our major deficits. Over the past four years the public has noticed that has ideology is more important to him than to the future our country. No one will listen to the President as long as he objects to his addiction!

With over $17 billion reaching higher and out of sight, the Obamas have spent over 44 million dollars in tax payers money on travel and associated expenditures. This is, without a doubt, the most traveled, and the most expensive president in our nations past. In March 2014 the president took 31 trips since 2009 which cost millions of dollars. In comparison Bush spent 116 days and Clinton 113 days and Reagan spent 73 days on just 14 days!

Accordingly, the mainstream media has President Obama by the short hairs because they refuse to demand transparency and accountability. Transparency or clear, obvious and accountability defined as responsible or liable, the American people are enduring the harsh realities of his viewing everything in relation to oneself!

THE ARTICLE OF IMPEACHMENT

The Article of Impeachment is for our 44th President, Barack Hussein Obama which is based on something that drags behind him of abuses over the past five years. Many different drafts will modify those already written.

The status of impeachment is clearly stated in this process and the particulars will be exhibited by the Senate:

> "ARTICLES OF IMPEACHMENT EXHIBITED BY THE HOUSE OF REPRESENTATIVES OF THE UNITED STATES IN THE NAME OF ITSELF AND ALL OF THE PEOPLE OF THE UNITED STATED OF AMERICA, AGAINST BARACK HUSSEIN OBAMA, PRESIDENT OF THE UNITED STATES OF AMERICA, IN MAINTENANCE AND SUPPORT OF ITS IMPEACHMENT AGAINST HIM FOR HIGH AND CRIMES AND MISDEMEANOURS". 68

1. He has through his subordinates allowed the specific systematic employment of the Internal Revenue Service while violating these rights

of citizens by the sole purpose of those groups obtaining tax-exempt status.

2. By his own techniques he has allowed the knowledge of Internal Revenue Service targeting political opponents so as not to have such knowledge be revealed during 2012 or in an election year.

3. He has allowed confidential material contained data which cannot for purposes not authorized by law. These may be income tax audits or other deemed investigations conducted in a bias manner.

4. He has lied to the American people regarding the time and development of the terrorist attack on Benghazi, Libya.

5. He treated badly the Department of Justice by violating the constitution rights of its citizens by destroying the real Department which should enforce the United States. Instead he takes control of passing laws passed by Congress and signed by a previous President, allowing the Attorney General to conduct surveillance of the media, "Fast and Furious" failed program, a goal of making a gun-control program which resulted in deaths of both American and Mexican citizens.

6. By his own actions his appointed Czars have promoted or suggested 932 Executive Orders in 40 months. The Senate does nothing nor even a budget or allowing any House bill being passed or even considered.

7. He, the President of the United States, has led through paltering in his Obamacare, National Security, Internal Revenue and foreign policies that has turned on his ability to lead this country.

An ordinary weakling compared with the ruler of Crimea with the exerciting of the United States and find our emperor weak to a point of deserting a loss of the essential strength of President Obama.

An ordinary weakling has already turned a once respected USA into a joke; reduce Congress to a sniveling crowd; turn the world's finest medical system into a third-rate nightmare with a stroke of writing equipment; snatch our Constitution without prompted recourse by frontiersman and pioneers was used to write that exact document and turn our once-United States into a group of completing assholes. We are afraid to fore fill this cause to place on the government teat should raise his voice to protect the win of the United States of America!

So don't slander the nonentity ruler has an agent that translates his uncertain ancestry and incompetence to do what king or dictator has done: destroy our 232 year history. President Obama has destroyed our founding fathers of America.

Epilogue

"Step by small step ...

In Hitler's Germany they watched as they came for the Jews.

In Hitler's Germany they watched as they came for the Gypsies.

In Hitler's Germany they watched as they came for their neighbors.

In Hitler's Germany when they came for them...it was too late.

When I finished reading this I was short of breath.

Looking back through the past four years, many "Whens" pop up. Read them all to better understand where we are going as a country.

WHEN – he refused to disclose who donated money to his election campaign, as other candidates had done, people said it didn't matter.

WHEN- he received endorsements from people like Louis Farrakhan, Muramar Kaddafi and Hugo Chavez, people said it didn't matter.

WHEN - it was pointed out that he was a total newcomer and had absolutely no experience at anything except community organizing, people said it didn't matter.

WHEN - he chose friends like acquaintances such as Bill Ayers and Bernadine Dohran, who were revolutionary radicals people said it didn't matter.

WHEN - his voting record in the Illinois Senate and in the US Senate came into question, people said it didn't matter.

WHEN - he refused to wear a flag lapel pin and did so only a public outcry, people said it didn't matter.

WHEN - people started treating him as a Messiah, and children in schools were taught to sing his praises, people said it didn't matter.

WHEN - he stood with his hands over his groin area for the playing of the National Anthem and pledge of Allegiance, people said it didn't matter.

WHEN - he surrounded himself in the White House with advisors who were pro-gun control, pro-abortion, pro-homosexual marriage, and wanting to curtail freedom of speech to silence the opposition, people said it didn't matter.

WHEN - he said he favors sex education in kindergarten, including homosexual indoctrination, people said it didn't matter.

WHEN - his personal background was either scrubbed or hidden and nothing could be found about him, people said it didn't matter.

WHEN - the place of his birth was called into question, and he refused to produce a birth certificate, people said it didn't matter.

WHEN - he had an association in Chicago with Tony Rezko a man of questionable character and who is now in prison and had helped Obama to a sweet deal on the purchase of his home, people said it didn't matter.

WHEN — it became known that George Soros, a multi-billionaire Marxists, spent a ton of money to get him elected, people said it didn't matter.

\WHEN - he started appointing White House Czars that were radical revolutionaries, and even allowed Marxist-Communists, people said it didn't matter.

WHEN - he stood before the Nation and told us that his intentions were to "fundamentally transform this Nation" into something else, people said it didn't matter.

WHEN - it became known that he had trained ACORN workers in Chicago and served as an attorney for ACORN, people said it didn't matter.

WHEN - he appointed cabinet members and several advisors who were tax cheats and socialists, people said it didn't matter.

WHEN - he appointed a Science Czar, John Holdren, who believes in forced abortions, mass sterilizations and seizing babies from teen mothers, people said it didn't matter.

WHEN - he appointed Cass Sunstein as Regulatory Czar who believes in "Explicit Consent," harvesting human organs without family consent and allowing animals to be represented in court, while banning all hunting, people said it didn't matter.

WHEN - he appointed Kevin Jennings, a homosexual and organizer of a group called Gay, Lesbian, Straight, Education Network as Safe School Czar and it became known that he had a history of bad advice to teenagers, people said it didn't matter.

WHEN - he appointed Mark Lloyd as Diversity Czar who believes in curtailing free speech, taking from one and giving to another to spread the wealth, who supports Hugo Chavez, people said it didn't matter.

WHEN - Valerie Jarrett, an avowed socialist was selected as Obama's Senior White House Advisor, people said it didn't matter.

WHEN -Anita Dunn, White House Communications Director, said Mao Tse Tung was her favorite philosopher and the person she turned to most for inspiration, people said it didn't matter.

WHEN - he appointed Carol Browner, a well known socialists as Global Warming Czar, working on Cap and Trade as the Nation's largest tax, people said it didn't matter.

WHEN - he appointed Van Jones, an ex-con and avowed Communist as Green Energy Czar, who since had to resign when this was made known, people said it didn't matter.

WHEN -Tom Daschle, Obama's pick for Health and Human Services Secretary could not be confirmed because he was a tax cheat, people said it didn't matter.

WHEN - as President of the United States, he bowed to the King of Saudi Arabia, people said it didn't matter.

WHEN - he traveled around the World criticizing America and never once talking of her greatness, people said it didn't matter.

WHEN - his actions concerning the Middle East seemed to support the Palestinians over Israel, our long time ally, people said it didn't matter.

WHEN - he took American tax dollars to resettle thousands of Palestinians from Gaza to the United States, people said it didn't matter.

WHEN - he upset the Europeans by removing plans for missile defense systems against the Russians, people said it didn't matter.

WHEN - he played politics in Afghanistan by not sending troops early-on when the Field Commanders said they were necessary to win, people said it didn't matter.

WHEN - he started spending us into a debt that was so big we could not pay it off, people said it didn't matter.

WHEN - he took a huge spending bill under the guise of stimulus and used it to pay off organizations, unions, and individuals that got him elected, people said it didn't matter.

WHEN - he took over insurance companies, car companies, banks, and etc., people said it didn't matter.

WHEN - he took away student loans from the banks and put it through the government, people said it didn't matter.

WHEN - he claimed he was a Christian during the election and tapes were later made public that showed Obama speaking to a Muslim group stating "that he was raised a Muslim, was educated a Muslim, and is still a Muslim, people said it didn't matter.

WHEN - he set into motion a plan to take over the control of all energy in the United States through Cap & Trade, people said it didn't matter.

WHEN - he finally completed his transformation of America into a Socialist State, people woke up—-but it was too late. Add these one by one and you get a score that points to the fact that Barrack Hussein Obama is determined to turn America into a Marxist- Socialist Society. All of the items in the proceeding paragraphs have been put into place. All can be documented very easily. Before you disavow this do an Internet search. The last paragraph alone is not yet cast in stone, you and I will write that paragraph. Will it read as above or will it be a happy ending for most of America?

Don't just belittle the opposition. Search for the truth. We all need to pull together or watch the demise of a free democratic society. We need to seek the truth and take action, for it will keep us FREE. Our biggest enemy is not China. Russia, North Korea, or Iran. Our biggest enemy is our complacent selves. The government will not help so we need to do it ourselves.

Question...will you pass this on to others who don't know about Obama's actions and plans for the USA, so that we may know how to vote in November 2014 and the ensuing years? Do you think it matters???

END NOTES

1. "Mitt Romney." Wikipedia. *en.wikipedia.org/wiki/Mitt_rommey*. June 25, 2013.

2. Anderson, James W. "Twelve reasons why I voted Demoncratic." *web.mail.comcast.net/zimbra/h/printmessage?-id/396340&tz=America/New_York&xim=1*. February 2, 2013.

3. Porter. John. "Obama's Second Term Transformation Plans." *web.mail.comasct.net/zimbra/h/printmessage?id=351900&tz=America_York &xim=1*. September 24, 2012.

4. "Conservatives Struggle to Explain How Mitt Rommey Lost 2012 Presidential Election." *www.huffingtonpost.com/2012/11/09/conservations-mitt-rommey-presidential-election_11_2099504.htm*. The Washington Post. January 30, 2013.

5. "Top-11, Only in America Obervations- by a Canadian, Only in America." *web.mail.comcast.net/zimbra/h/printmessage?id=393660&tz=America/New_York&xim=1*, January 23, 2013.

6. "Yemen." Wikipedia. *en.wikipedia.org/wiki/Yemen*. November 15, 2013.

7. "Syria." Wikipedia.

8. Marro, Ryan. "Satellite Photos Support Testimony That Iraqi: WMD Went To Syria." June 6, 2010. *http://pjmedia.com/blog.satellite-photos-support testimony-that-iraqi wmb- went -to-Syria*. December 29, 2012.

9. Ibid.

10. Ibid.

11. Ibid.

12. Ibid.

13. O'Brien, Michael. "US Offers Syrian rebels Military Support, alleges Assad used chemical weapons." NBC News. *nbcpolitics.nbc.com/_news/2013/06/13/18940169-us-offers-strian-rebels-military-suppopt-alleges-assad-used-chemical-weapons?lite*. June 7, 2013.

14. "Iran." Wikipedia.
15. Gayathri, Amrutha. "Egypt Crisis: US To Deliver F16 fighter Jets to Egypt's Military As Part of Defense Aid." July 26, 2013.
16. Sekulow, Jay. "American Center for Law and Justice, No US F16's for Egypt: Middle East Turmoil." *ACJL ACLJ.org/middle-east-turmoil/jay-sekulow-no-us-warplanes-to-muslim-brotherhood*. August 25, 2013.
17. Gertz, Bill. "Russia Akula Submarine." Washington Free Press. *congressmontomtoncredo.com/tag/russia*. November 8, 2012.
18. Hoffman, David. "Putin's Career Rooted in Russia's KGB." *www.washingtonpost.com/srv/intati/longterm/russiagov/putin.htm*. January 30, 2000.
19. Dvorack, Kimberly Y. "Did a Russian sub patrol the Gulf of Mexico unbeknowst to the US?" *www.examiner.com/article/evesion-sub-patrols-gulf-of-mexico-unbeknowst-to-us*. November 8, 2012.
20. Faal, Sorcha. "Russia Issued Apocalyptic Warning for the US Gulf Coast." *www.Whatdoesit mean.com/index1607.htm*. November 8, 2012.
21. "Health Care In The United States." Wikipedia. *en.wikipedia.org/wiki/Health=care-in-the-United/States*. July 26, 2013.
22. Sebelius, Kathleen. The Washington Post. January 16, 2014.
23. Ibid.
24. Altman, Drew. "No Quick Verdict on Obamacare." *www.polito.com/2013/09/no-quick-verdict-on-obamacare-97561.htm1*.
25. Beck, Glenn. "Obamacare Official admits: 60 to 70 percent of Healthcare.gov still need to be built." *www.glennbeck.com/2013/11/20/obamacare-official-admits-60-to-70-percent-of- healthcare-gov-still-needs-to-be-built/?utm_source=Daily&utm_medicine=emails&*.
26. "2012 Benghazi Attack." Wikipedia. *en.wikipedia.org/wiki/2012_Benghazi_attack*.
27. Kiely, Eugene. "Benghazi Timeline." *factcheck.org/2012/10/benghazi-timeline*.
28. Handley, Phil "Hands", Colonel, USAF (Ret). "Betrayal in Benghazi." *web.mail.comcast.net/zimbra/h/printmessage?id=475579&tz=Ameriac/New_York&xim=1*. September 18, 2013.
29. Beck, Glenn. "Benghazi: Was a 'Stand Down' Order Given?" *www.glennbeck.com/2013/06/07/exclusive-was-a-stand-down-order-given?utm_source=Daily&utm_medium=email&utm_campaign=2013-05=07=218647&utm_co*.
30. Griffen, Drew; and Kathleen Johnson. "CIA operators to testify at classified Benghazi hearing." *www.c.n.n.com/2013/1031/politics/benghazi-cia-hearing/index.htm1*. October 31, 2013.
31. Schmitt, Eric. "After Benghazi Attack, Talk Lagged Behind Intelli-

gence." *www.nytimes.com/2012/10/22/us/politics/explanation/for/benghazi-attack-under-scruitiny.html?pagewanted=all.*

32. Beck, Glenn. "WH Spokesperson stumped: Where was Obama on the night of Beneghazi attack?" September 18, 2013.

33. "Hillary Rodham Clinton's Tenure as Secretary of State." Wikipedia.*en.wikipedia.org/wiki/Hillary_Rodman_Clinton%27_tenure/as/Secretary_of_St ate.*

34. Garrison, Dean. "15 More Benghazi-Related Victums Murdered: Does it Matter Now Hillary?" Accessed on January 16, 2014. *www.newsmax.com/surveys.* January 17, 2014.

35. Howerton, Jason. "GOP Rep. Reads Previously Released Benghazi Email During Hearing, Whisteeblower says he was stunned Attack was blamed on video." *www:the blaze.com/stories/2013/13/05/08.rep-Trey-Gowdy-reads-previous-unreleased-benghazi-email-during-whisteblower-says-he-was embassassed-att.* May 11, 2013.

36. Colon, Alicia. "Obama Would Be Toast If Americans Actually Paid Attention To Benghazi." *www.irishexmanierusa.com/2013/06/04/obama_would_be_toast_if_americ.html.*

37. Ulsterman, Admiral James Lyons. "We Need Full Disclosure on Benghazi NOW." *web.mail.comcast.net/zimbra/h/printmessage?id=364680&tz-America/New_York&xim-1.* September 4, 2013.

38. "2013 IRS Scandal." Wikipedia. *en.wikipedia.org/wiki/2013_IRS_scandal.* September 17, 2013.

39. Beck, Glenn. "IRS Scandal: Lois Lerner pleads the fifth." *www.glennbeck.com/2013/05/22/irs-scandal-lois-lerner-pleads-the-fifth?utm_soorce-Daily&utm_medium=email&utm_conf.* May 22, 2013.

40. Ibid.

41. Ibid.

42. Viguerie, Richard. "Isn't It Time to Arrest Lois Lerner?"_1_ConservativeHQ.com.* March 6, 2014.

43. Reed, Dr. Ralph. "Stop Omaba War on Conservatives and Christians, Red State Advacary, Faith and Freedom Coalition." *red-state@news.red-state.com.* February 24, 2014.

44. "National Security Agency." Wikipedia. *en.wikipedia.org/wiki/National_Security_Agency.* October 3, 2013.

45. MacAskill, Eiven; Julian Borger; and Glenn Greenwald. "The National Security Agency: surveillance giant with eyes on America." *www.the guardian.com/world/2013/jun/06/national-security-agency-surveillance.* October 3, 2013.

46. Fidel, Steve. "Utah's $1.5 billion cyber-security center-under way."

www.desertnews.com/article/705363940/Utaha-15-billion-cyber-security-center-under-way.html?pq=all. October 8, 2013.

47. Cook, Josha. "NSA Ant Spy Gear: A Secret Weapon that Hacks Electronics Worldwide." *freedamoutpost.com/2013/12/nsa-ant-spy-gear-secret-weapon-hacks-electronics-worldwide.* December 31, 2013.

48. Swann, Ben. "Federal Judge: NSA Spying is Legal- Ruling Based on Emotion, Not Law." *freedomoutpost.com/2013/12/federal-judge-nsa-spying-legal-ruling-based-emotion-law.* December 31, 2013.

49. Livingstone, Bob. "What's Behind Obama's Military Purge?"*web.mail.comcast.net/zimbra/printmessage?id=443201&tz=American/New_York&xim=1.*

50. Spenser, Jack."The Facts About Military Readiness" September 15, 2000.

51. Livingstone, Bob. "What's Behind Obama's Military Purge?" Accessed on November 16, 2013. *personalliberty.com/2012/11/16/whats-behind-obama's-military purge/.* February 19, 2012.

52. Beck, Glenn. "Obama's about-face on the sequester." Accessed on February 20, 2013. *www.glenbeck.com/2013/02/20/obama's-about-face-on-the-sequester/?utm_source=Daily&utm_medium=email&utm_campaign=2013-2-20_201024&utm_conte.*

53. Secretary of the Navy Ray Mabus, Department of the Navy Response to the Sequestration, March 2, 2012.

54. Beres, Robin. "Cuts jeopardize national security." Richmond Times Dispatch Editorial, March 28, 2013.

55. Wong, Kristina. "Pentagon budget slashed benefits." *http://thehill.com/blogs/defeon-hill/budget-appropriation/199050-hagel-unveils-basics-of-2015-defense-budget-request#ix222uJIzDeVy.* February 24, 2014.

56. "Department of Homeland Security." Wikipedia. *en.wikipedia.org/wiki/Homeland_security.* May 15, 2014.

57. Whitehead, John. "Homeland Security: America's Standing Army." *newsmax.com.* June 28, 2014.

58. Hestilow, Captain Terry M., USA, Retired.*to,ferrandez20.com/2013/11/18/retired-army-officer-warns-dhs-preparing-for-war-against-american-citizens.* March 30, 2013.

59. "Barack Obama Citizenship Conspiracy theories." Wikipedia. May 15, 2011.

60. Veroto, Gace. "Forensic findings on Obama's birth certificate: A100 percent forgery, no doubt about it." *www.worldtribne.com/2013/07/08/forigic-findings-on-obamas-birth-certificate-a-100-percent-forgery-no-doubt-about-it.* July 5, 2013.

61. "Occidemtial College Transcripts provide concrete evidence to annul Obama Presidency." *presscore.ca/2012/obama-occidental-college-transcripts-provides-concrete-evidence-that-annuls-his-prsidency.html*. October 14, 2012.

62. Ibid.

63. Ibid.

64. Thomas, Michael. "Obama's Birth Certificate: Confirmed Forgery According To Top Experts." *www.storyleak.comobama-birth certificate-confirmed-forgery, genealogy.com/Birth+Records*.

65. Jackson, Victoria. "Mysterious Death Related To Omaba's Fake Birth Certificate." *victoriajackson.com/10252/mysterious-death-related-obama-fake-birth=certificate*. December 13, 2013.

66. Ibid.

67. Sunday Standard, Kenya Obama all set for US Senate, 2004Flashback-Kenyan Newspaper Reported Barak Obama Born in Kenya: FreedomOutpost , May 19, 2014

68. Elliott, Steve. "The Case To Impeach." *www.grassfire.com*, 2013.

69. Mekton, Melissa. "House Has Enough Votes to Impeach.... And." *newsmax.com/surveys*. June 19, 2014.